Political Gladiators

How Millennials Can Navigate the 21st Century

Political Minefield and WIN!

by

Joshua A. Lafazan

AUSTIN • DALLAS • NEW YORK • PHILADELPHIA • SAN FRANCISCO

Next Gen Publishing
PermissionCoordinator@NextGenPublishing.org
Team@NextGenPublishing.org
SpecialSalesDepartment@NextGenPublishing.org
www.NextGenPublishing.org

Printed in the United States of America.

Ordering information:
Quantity sales. Special discounts are available on quantity purchases by corporations, associations, and others. For details, contact the 'Special Sales Department' at the address above.

Political Gladiators: How Millennials Can Navigate the 21st Century Political Minefield and WIN! First edition.

ISBN-13: 978-0692592083
ISBN-10: 0692592083

Life shrinks or expands in proportion to one's courage.

-Anaïs Nin

To Dad,

      For my father; everything I am, and everything I will ever have is because of you. From early Saturday mornings on the baseball field, to afternoons on the campaign trail, to late nights helping me with speeches and position papers, you've been my rock for as long as I can remember. You showed me the definition of hard work, and how there's no substitute for it. You taught me about the importance of having integrity in everything you say and do. You helped me find my passion, and never let me shy away from my dreams despite how much they scare me at times. Thank you for always telling me what I need to hear, rather than what I want. Thank you for picking me up and dusting me off whenever I'm down. Most importantly, thank you for showing me that being a man means being there for your kids, and always making Justin, Aaron, and me your life's priority. I can only hope to one day instill in my own children the lessons, the passion, and the morals you've instilled in me. I love you, dad.

<u>To Mom,</u>

For my mother; the person who understands me like no other in this world, and the person I call my best friend. You are a woman who deserves infinite praise, yet asks for none. You are a woman who goes to great lengths to help others, yet requires no reciprocity. You are a woman with such enduring strength, and vast compassion. You are a woman who deserves a medal for raising three energetic, opinionated, and boisterous boys (mostly Aaron). Thank you for always picking up the phone whenever I need you. Thank you for always listening and for knowing precisely what to say to make me feel better about whatever situation I find myself in. Thank you for continually going out of your way, whether cancelling plans to take me to an event, or dropping off forgotten homework at school, and without question putting me first. Thank you for always instructing me to "stay in my own lane," and to focus on the work at hand instead of the distractions from the outside world. Most importantly, thank you for setting the standard on qualities I will look for in a life partner; a woman who embodies motherhood with the commitment and the passion that you do. I love you, mom.

Table of Contents

Introduction: 1

Chapter 1: Why are you Running for Office? - 7

Chapter 2: A Difficult Endeavor - 42

Chapter 3: Walk Before You Run - 57

Chapter 4: It's All About the Issues - 76

Chapter 5: The Campaign - 94

Chapter 6: Impact on Your Life - 173

Chapter 7: Lessons Learned - 186

Quick Links: 201

Meet America's Young Elected Officials: 202

About the Author: 224

Acknowledgements

Actress Emma Roberts once said, "I'm surrounded by great friends and family. I don't know what I would do without them." Seldom has a quote more accurately captured the way I feel about those who touch my life; I don't know where I would be without you.

There are so many people to thank. But, first, I thank the Syosset community, to whom I owe everything. You took a chance on me when I was an 18-year-old neophyte, and had my back when adversity struck, and you continue to encourage me to this day. I will never take your support for granted. I solemnly swear to never forget where I came from; once a Syosset Brave—always a Syosset Brave!

I want to thank the people who are entirely and unequivocally responsible for the man I am today—my parents Sandy and Jeff Lafazan. My younger brothers Justin, Aaron, and I always say that as we've entered adulthood, we realize that we had the least to do with our success. We had what could be argued as an unfair advantage—incredible parents. Our parents are far from perfect, and our family is still learning how to best support one another, but the principles our parents taught us have remained constant throughout our so far short lives—leadership, integrity, curiosity, and courage. My only hope in life is to make them both proud.

My brothers are my best friends in the world, and I want to thank them for their unwavering support throughout every new endeavor I take on in my life. Whether it was helping me launch Safe Ride Syosset off the ground in 2011, or assisting with my campaign in 2012, or accompanying me to one charity luncheon after the next in 2013, aiding with college applications in 2014, and lending a hand for this book in 2015, you both showed up. I never have to worry, as I know you are always by my side. Justin and Aaron, I love you both limitlessly. Also Justin, I'm taking this moment to formally apologize as requested; I'm sorry for that one time we played *Rock Band* when we were kids, and you were so bad at the drums that we didn't move up a level and I proceeded to ignore you for three weeks. My bad!

I want to thank my "Big Red" family at Cornell University for embracing me with open arms when I stepped on campus fall 2014. Transferring to Cornell was undoubtedly one of the best decisions I have made. Studying at Cornell is an incredible privilege, and one that I'm immensely grateful for. To everyone I've met—from the group of friends I made during orientation week, to my ILR classmates, to my Alpha Epsilon Pi fraternity brothers—you've all touched my life regardless of the scope of our interaction. I thank you from the bottom of my heart for making Ithaca feel like a second home.

Without the dedicated volunteers from my 2012 campaign, I would have had zero chance of winning the election. There are too many individuals to thank from the vast army of volunteers. However, a couple of people truly went above and beyond for me. Thank you to my Campaign Manager Myles Blodnick who stood in front of supermarkets for hours distributing literature, and, no doubt, knocked on as many doors as I did. I appreciate all of your efforts. Thank you to Barbara Bonomi for braving the New York winter to gather signatures for me; Ms. Bonomi, who passed away in 2012, you will never be forgotten. Thank you to Zach Hammer, Theo Martin, Jake Asman, and Dan Budick for bringing my campaign into the 21st century and making our school board campaign one of the most tech-savvy in the nation. Thank you to Alex Rosenblatt,

Michael Starr, Alex Kugelman, and Jared Swedler for standing on Jericho Turnpike with a big sign: "Lafazan for Board of Ed" (sorry about the cars that honked at you!). Thank you to Anthony Leo for driving me around all those late nights at 3:00 a.m. to put up lawn signs. Thank you to Stuart Varney for having me on FOX Business Network's "Varney & Co.," and allowing me to tell my story. Thank you to New York State Comptroller Tom DiNapoli for your sage advice and counsel early in my campaign. Thank you to each one of my friends and neighbors who knocked on doors, handed out a piece of literature, displayed a lawn sign, spoke with a neighbor, or did something above and beyond to promote my campaign; to have had your support is humbling beyond measure.

An enormous thank goes out to all who went on television to refute the lies that were being disseminated by the school district about my family and me on the day before my first election in 2012. (I will elaborate on this later.) You stopped the tide of negativity before any damage and I'm eternally grateful for all of you.

Thank you to my editor, Mary Ellen Walsh, for your stewardship during this entire process. You've believed in me since our very first meeting in Starbucks in 2014, all the way through the completion of this book. I'm forever grateful for your help (and patience!).

Thank you to my amazing designer and close friend, Matthew Alessandri, for your amazing work. I'll always cherish the late-night eats at Hurricane Grill in Syosset going over numerous design strategies, and I'll always be appreciative your meticulous approach to this book design.

I'm blessed to have a wealth of mentors in my life. What I might lack in life experience that comes with age, I make up for with sound advice from a small group of individuals who are so important to me. Thank you to United States Surgeon General Regina M. Benjamin, NY GOP Chairman Ed Cox, Assemblywoman Nicole Malliotakis, Nassau County Executive Ed Mangano, Dr. Jeffrey Reynolds, Brian Nevin, Adam Haber, David Schwartz, Brad Gerstman, Paul Annunziato, Ginger Lieberman, Dr. Thomas Rogers, Dr. Ronald Friedman, Dr. Steve Chassman, Jon Cooper, and Dr. Luvelle Brown.

Lastly, I want to thank *you* for taking the time to read my book. Whether you're a political enthusiast, or you abhor politics with the same passion as you do morning traffic and mosquito bites, taking the time to read this book means the world to me. I hope you enjoy it!

Letter from the Author

I first decided to run for office during my sophomore year at Syosset High School located on the North Shore of Long Island, NY. Because I was an avid student of local politics and government, I was cognizant of the unrest in the community when it came to the lack of transparency and open government policy practices with members of the Syosset School Board. (I will expand on this shortly). Having seen our superintendent plastered monthly on the front page of *Newsday*, Long Island's big daily newspaper, I was keenly aware that Syosset residents were tired of having the highest paid administrator in the State of New York—$506,322 in total compensation.[1] This angered many residents who couldn't fathom how a superintendent of a district with 6,600 students could make more than the President of the United States. Something my parents instilled in me at a young age, and what I hope to instill in every young person I meet, is that age is NOT a prerequisite to become a leader. If the current Syosset School Board was not best serving the public, then why couldn't I be an effective trustee on the board? Why would being a teenager disqualify me from being able to advocate for those things the community clearly wanted and our students needed?

I'll never forget coming home on a Sunday afternoon in the spring of 2010 and letting my parents know the news; I decided that I wanted to run for office as a trustee for our school board. The reactions of my parents were completely different. My father the risk taker was 100% on board. He greeted me with a smile and said, "Josh, there's no doubt in my mind that you can do this."

---

[1] "She's in a cla$$ by herself | New York Post." 2013. 19 Oct. 2015 <http://nypost.com/2011/03/06/shes-in-a-cla-by-herself/>

Boy that was the easy part. I would later have to tell my mother, the pragmatist of my family and the person who keeps my father in check! She approached me with important questions that I hadn't yet thought of, such as: how would this affect my college plans, what specific qualifications were needed to run, and whether I would need to align with a political party. But she quickly realized I was serious, and, like she tells me every single day of my life, said, "If you're all-in, then we're all-in."

I will speak about this later in the book, but running for office is absolutely a family affair. I'm blessed that my family has had my back and has not wavered in their support from that very Sunday afternoon in 2010. Your family is a resource both for support and sage advice. They are the best sounding board for ideas, to pick you up when you're down, and no matter how aggravated they can become sometimes, they will always be your easiest votes!

Flash forward to 2015 where I had been re-elected for another three-year term to the Syosset School Board of Education! This afternoon, in the board of education conference room in Syosset's South Woods Middle School, I will take the Oath of Office to begin my second term on the board.

In between classes and research papers, I wrote a significant portion of this book from the confines of my dorm room at Cornell University where I am a senior in the ILR School.

I believe all elected officials should lead by example in serving their communities in both public offices and other capacities. Community is everything to me, and I spend the majority of my time working towards making it a better place to live, especially when it comes to three issues of paramount importance: education reform, the scourge of drug and alcohol addiction, and matters facing Long Island, New York's youth. As a member of the Syosset School Board of Education, I lead efforts to bring 21st-century-education reforms to the classroom, and include cost-saving measures to help protect taxpayers. As a board member of the Long Island Council on Alcoholism and Drug Dependence, and a member of the Nassau County Heroin Prevention Task Force, I work towards the elimination of heroin and prescription drug abuse on Long Island. As a board member of the Nassau County Youth Board of Directors, and a member of the Long Island Youth Safety Coalition, I help develop solutions to keep the youth of Long Island safe from the dangers facing them in the 21st century. Lastly, I'm proud to serve as a volunteer firefighter in the Varna Volunteer Fire Department in upstate New York.

I chose to write this book for many reasons, but none more important than this; there are simply not enough tools available for young candidates to help guide them during their campaigns. When I ran for the Syosset School Board in 2012, the only information available were news articles from a Google search: "18 year old runs for school board." I was fortunate to have had an exceptional "brain trust" of advisors to rely on, such as a school board member from a neighboring town, several people who had run for office themselves, and the New York State Comptroller, combined with a dedicated group of campaign volunteers who I will forever be in debt to for turning my campaign into a movement for change. Through the telling of my story, fused with the stories of other young elected officials from across the country, I aim to give you the best picture of what running for office as a young candidate looks like. My greatest hope is that this book inspires you to run for office, and gives you the tools necessary to be successful on Election Day.

Josh Lafazan
Syosset, NY
June 29, 2015

<u>Introduction</u>

It was nearing 11 p.m. on the night of May 15, 2012: Election Day for school board candidates across New York. Though the torrential downpours of the day had made for a cool night in Syosset, Long Island, New York, the cafeteria of South Woods Middle School where the election results were being announced felt like a blazing inferno. I was sweating and pacing nervously in my full suit and tie, the same outfit that I planned on wearing to prom the next month.

In the moments just before this announcement, everything stood still. Though I was surrounded by about 300 classmates, friends, and supporters in a crowded cafeteria electrified with energy equal to a Knicks playoff game at Madison Square Garden, an unnerving silence came over me. After two full years of planning and preparation, trial and error, and triumphs and disappointments, the wildest journey I could have ever imagined was about to conclude. This was the moment I had been waiting for.

I stood in the middle of the cafeteria with my two best friends, Greg Morley and Justin Cristando. Greg is that friend who always provides comic relief when it's needed most. Noticing how much I was sweating, he whispered to me, "Win or lose, please take a shower as soon as you get home!" Right on cue, this definitely elicited a laugh from me. He then followed with, "There's no doubt in my mind you're going to win, bud...I'm so proud of you." Justin, the eternal optimist, turned to me, put a hand on my shoulder and let me know that, "No matter what happens, you've inspired this entire town and young people all over. You got this, man."

Five candidates were vying for three trustee seats on the Syosset School Board of Education in 2012. For those of you who may not know what a school board of education is, it's the group of people who govern the educational system of a school district. In New York, all members who serve on a school board have the title of "trustee."

Only two incumbents were running, as Trustee Shari Dorfman chose not to seek re-election. In ballot position number one was Christopher DiFilippo, an independent information technology project manager. DiFilippo, 58, was a volunteer emergency medical technician at the Syosset Fire Department. In ballot position number two was Dr. Alan Resnick, an anesthesiologist. Resnick, 48, was a three-year incumbent running for re-election. In ballot position number three was Jon Moore, 40, who worked for Carrier Corporation, a subsidiary of United Technologies. Moore was president of the CYO Youth Sports Program in Syosset. In ballot position number four was Sonia Rutigliano, the owner of Jack and Rose Florist in Woodbury. Rutigliano, 58, was also a three-year incumbent running for re-election. While DiFilippo was running as an individual, Resnick, Moore, and Rutigliano were running as a team.

Candidates with the three highest vote tallies would be elected to the board. 2,531, 2,474, 2,365, and 2,115 votes had already been announced for candidates on ballot lines #1-4. I vividly recall that my heart beat a full foot outside of my chest as Vice President April Neuendorf was set to announce the final vote total for the candidate on ballot line #5: Joshua A. Lafazan.[2]

---

[2] "Syosset Votes 18-Year-Old to School Board | Patch." 2014. 20 Oct. 2015
<http://patch.com/new-york/syosset/difilippo-lafazan-resnick-win-boe-election-budget-passes>

Though I could barely stand still from anxiousness (If I was wearing a pedometer, the number would have easily surpassed six digits from constant pacing), I felt at peace; I had given every last ounce of energy that I had to my campaign. Being a trustee on the school board was a position that I wanted with every fiber of my being. Whatever the outcome, I would accept it.

From that Sunday afternoon in 2010 when I first told my parents I was going to run, and my formal announcement of my campaign in 2011, to filing paperwork and actually running in 2012, to this very moment in time, I had no regrets; I gave it everything I had.

Neuendorf paused, then looked up. As my gaze danced excitedly across the room, I locked eyes with my dad. He gave me a wink, always reminding me that my parents had my back. Out of the corner of my eye I saw one of my closest friends, Nikhil Goyal, shoot me a thumbs up and smile as Neuendorf began to announce my vote tally.

The total began with the number 4, and before the remaining three digits could even be announced, the cafeteria broke out into deafening cheers of sheer pandemonium.

I had done it!

I had been elected to the Syosset School Board of Education! My heart was pounding at a million beats per minute, and I was beaming from ear to ear. At age 18, I had just made history and became one of the youngest elected officials in the annals of New York State.

I was instantly rushed by a jubilant crowd of my classmates in what was, to date, the greatest celebration of my life. The group erupted so loudly, that I would only later learn that my exact vote tally was 4,739. As the *Syosset Patch,* AOL's hyper-local news outlet, would shortly publish, I had captured 82% of the vote—one of the largest victories in Syosset School Board electoral history.

*

Yes, there are an abundance of books and articles already available that advise candidates on how to run campaigns. But that information is mainly applicable to adult candidates; young candidates play in an entirely different arena. Young candidates almost always have their motives questioned. Adults don't share the same scrutiny. While young candidates are routinely criticized for lack of experience, adult candidates are heralded for their experience. Lastly, while young candidates are immediately surrounded by a cloud of doubt over whether they can actually emerge victorious in a campaign, adult candidates are expected to win by default.

Young candidates seem to climb an uphill battle.

Due to these challenges, young candidates often get discouraged from running, or they run and lose because they cannot overcome the difficult path of being the youngest candidate in a race. Countless candidates such as Austin Ogden for the Dublin School Board in California in 2012, Teddy McCullough for the Lopez Island School Board in Washington in 2013, and Steven Meyer for the New York State Assembly in 2014 courageously ran against established adult candidates and lost.

It is often forgotten that America was founded by disruptive youth; four of our nation's Founding Fathers were in their 20s during the Constitutional

Convention.[3] Yet America has largely abandoned the inclusion of youth into the nation's most important policy conversations. Millennials, though the largest demographic in the United States as of 2015 with 75.3 million, surpassing the Baby Boomers with 74.9 million, are the most underrepresented age group in government today.[4] We are the most educated and the most diverse generation in American history, but our voices aren't heard; we've mustered a lousy 2% of seats in the U.S. House of Representatives (9 out of 435).[5]

Millennials also rarely serve on school boards. School boards of education, governmental bodies charged with making policies and decisions about students, are vastly comprised of adults from previous generations. Who would better know which policies are working and which ones aren't and what needs amending more than the students governed by these policies? Who better to know which programs are beneficial and which need replacing more than students who participate in them? Who better to both represent and articulate the needs of students more than a student or a recent graduate?

It's time to change this.

It's time that we, as a generation, begin to take ourselves seriously and rise to the challenge of shaping

---

[3] "The Right to Run - Slate." 2014. 20 Oct. 2015
<http://www.slate.com/articles/news_and_politics/politics/2014/10/age_of_candidacy_laws_should_be_abolished_why_18_year_olds_should_be_able.html>

[4] "This year, Millennials will overtake Baby Boomers | Pew ..." 2015. 2 Nov. 2015 <http://www.pewresearch.org/fact-tank/2015/01/16/this-year-millennials-will-overtake-baby-boomers/>

[5] "This year, Millennials will overtake Baby Boomers | Pew ..." 2015. 2 Nov. 2015 <http://www.pewresearch.org/fact-tank/2015/01/16/this-year-millennials-will-overtake-baby-boomers/>

the America that will be our reality for decades to come. The first step is getting involved. Whether you're running for your local school board, your town council, or a seat in your state legislature, rarely will you ever encounter a better opportunity to effect real and meaningful change. Less talk and more action. It's time to get off the bench, and get into the game. It's show time.

Why Are You Running for Office?

The first step of any campaign is to make the decision to run. This holds true for any office—from a local village trustee seat to the presidency of the United States; major news outlets spent months having pundits debate whether politicians such as Joe Biden or Hillary Clinton would enter the 2016 White House race. So you've made your decision; think long and hard—why are you throwing your hat into the ring? You will have to answer this question each and every day of your campaign. Running for office will be the most challenging adventure you partake in. **Campaigning is hard. Holding an elected office may be even harder.** There is a serious responsibility to holding that office. You no longer will be just a citizen; you'll be a public servant.

Nicole Malliotakis is among the youngest lawmakers in the New York State Assembly. She calls being an elected official, "One of most challenging jobs you can have." Moreover, she warns young candidates that, "You really have to want to do this. You have to have a passion or you won't do a good job." So think about it. Why do you want to run for office? What do you want to see changed? What is motivating you to beat the incumbent; to embrace the inevitable criticism and doubt that comes with being a young candidate and persevere in the face of adversity? What are your beliefs and core convictions?

Personally, I wanted to fight for open government and transparency in my community. I was a student at Syosset High School, a premier district in a New York hamlet on Long Island, home to about 20,000 residents with seven elementary schools, two middle schools, and a perennially ranked top-200 high school nationally.[6] From an outsider's perspective, things in Syosset were fine. However, in my eyes and the eyes of many other residents with or without children in the schools, Syosset was a gilded district; beneath the academic success of the student body was enormous community unrest. The disturbance in the community stemmed from two focal points: a highly-compensated superintendent, and a lack of openness in school district affairs. Dr. Carole Hankin was the superintendent of the Syosset Central School District from when I first stepped off the bus at Walt Whitman Elementary School in 1999 through my senior year at Syosset High. Dr. Hankin made Syosset infamous; her pay package of $506,322 was the highest in New York State.[7] Worse than her salary was the negative publicity she drew within the district. The *New York Post* inked a top story about Dr. Hankin with the title "She's in a Cla$$ By Herself."[8] Even New York State Governor Andrew Cuomo joined the chorus of criticism, joking in a budget address that he "applied for that job" and only ran for Governor upon his rejection from the post.[9] Yet while Dr. Hankin earned serious dough, she was not accessible to the people that funded her paycheck. Board agendas were secretive, public comment at board

---

[6] "Ten LI high schools among top 200 nationally in U.S. News ..." 2014. 20 Oct. 2015 <http://www.newsday.com/long-island/education/ten-li-high-schools-among-top-200-nationally-in-u-s-news-ranking-1.7794781>

[7] "She's in a cla$$ by herself | New York Post." 2013. 20 Oct. 2015 <http://nypost.com/2011/03/06/shes-in-a-cla-by-herself/>

[8] "She's in a cla$$ by herself | New York Post." 2013. 20 Oct. 2015 <http://nypost.com/2011/03/06/shes-in-a-cla-by-herself/>

[9] "Cuomo Criticizes School Officials' Salaries - The New York ..." 2011. 20 Oct. 2015 <http://www.nytimes.com/2011/02/07/nyregion/07cuomo.html>

meetings only allowed for questions on pre-determined items, and there was a pervasive fear of retribution for even thinking about running for a position on the board; there were uncontested elections for several years before I ran in 2012. Even today, more than two full years after Hankin has retired, scores of residents are still wary of going on the record to testify about or against her.

Hankin was CEO of Syosset's school system for 23 years. In a community whose pride stems from its outstanding schools, Hankin amassed major power in her position through the success of the school district. She accumulated several awards such as the "Kennedy Center Alliance for Arts Education Network and National School Boards Association Award of Excellence and the Magna Award."[10] Moreover, Hankin was given total control by the school board and community; she successfully passed budgets year after year, was able to pass multiple bond issuances, and was given carte blanche to increase her salary and pad her pay package with perks such as "$67,454 in fringe benefits and $52,000 in retirement funds and expenses including use of a 'late model car,' plus gas."[11]

Here was where my issues with the district took shape. One of the main responsibilities of a board of education is to employ a superintendent. Of course, negotiating a salary falls under this category. Yet I, along with hundreds of residents, felt that we had a superintendent who gave marching orders to the board

---

[10] "Dr. Hankin Wins State Arts Education Award - AntonNews.com." 2007. 20 Oct. 2015
<http://www.antonnews.com/syossetjerichotribune/2007/06/22/news/hankin.html>
[11] "She's in a cla$$ by herself | New York Post." 2013. 20 Oct. 2015
<http://nypost.com/2011/03/06/shes-in-a-cla-by-herself/>

of education. How else could the board justify the salary she received? How else could the board of education justify having members cast not one single "no" vote at public board meetings? How else could the board justify the policies and practices that shut the community out from participation? Clearly, the board of education was not running the show, and I knew in order to effect any real and meaningful change, this had to stop.

You may be leery as to the lengths a superintendent would go to control the school board of education. I was definitely in the dark myself, until it happened to me. In January of 2012, the AP government classes at Syosset High School had an assembly to listen to our Congressman, Representative Steve Israel.[12] After the assembly ended, I was asked to stay afterwards. In an empty auditorium, in the company of only Dr. Hankin and the principal of Syosset High School, Dr. Hankin made me an intriguing offer; should I forego running a negative campaign, which meant agreeing to NOT criticize her salary or her administration, she would not only endorse my candidacy but she would convince one of the incumbents to withdraw from running for re-election. Seldom in my life have I been more nervous than at that moment. I couldn't believe the offer put in front of me. I had just been handed the golden ticket to my dream of becoming one of the youngest elected officials in New York, yet I knew immediately in my gut that accepting this offer would be wrong. On one hand, my career would kick start effortlessly and I would be ensured victory without a fight. On the other hand, I would sacrifice my principles. I was raised by my mother and

---

[12] "Jan. 4: Congressman Visits Syosset High School | Patch." 2015. 4 Dec. 2015 <http://patch.com/new-york/syosset/jan-4-congressman-visits-syosset-high-school>

father to speak out for what I believed in and to always do the right thing as opposed to taking the easy way out. I wasn't sure how to reject her offer respectfully and told Dr. Hankin that I would think about it. A few days later, I rejected her offer. As I would later tell Stuart Varney when I appeared on FOX Business Network's "Varney & Co." after my election, "I will not be beholden to the closed power structure."[13] **Even if I lost, I would lose with the same level of integrity that I had in the beginning.**

   I've painted a pretty bleak picture for you of the state of affairs in Syosset in 2012. This is crucial because it helps to explain why I had the type of passionate support in my community that helped me win the election. For years people felt mistreated. For years taxpayers felt taken advantage of. I became the vehicle for residents to channel their anger. I was willing to take the task in what was dubbed a "David vs. Goliath" matchup.[14] Few thought I had a chance to win. Even fewer thought I would actually win a seat on the board. **Regardless of whether you're a neophyte candidate at 18, or a seasoned politician at 50, when your community has your back, the sky's the limit for what you can achieve.** I owe the Syosset community everything. And when it comes to community dynamics, I've learned two important lessons.

   First, I've come to realize that *most* adults and youths alike are afraid to lead, but they will

---

[13] "School District Head Paid $540K While Freezing Teachers ..." 3 Dec. 2015 <http://video.foxbusiness.com/v/1619486568001/school-district-head-paid-540k-while-freezing-teachers-pay/>

[14] "Syosset class prez seeks school board seat | Newsday." 20 Oct. 2015 <http://www.newsday.com/long-island/nassau/syosset-class-prez-seeks-school-board-seat-1.3688221>

follow, if lead by actions with a good message. I made a difference as an 18 year old by filling the void of leadership in my community. *Yes*, an 18 year old filled the void. Why? Because youthful enthusiasm coupled with honest intentions can be a powerful force in this world. We have not yet become jaded and pessimistic about the world. Use your youthful exuberance and your belief in your ideals to persevere and overcome all obstacles. Only you get to decide what are the limits of your energy and your desire to succeed.

Secondly, I've realized that many will complain in private, but few will speak up in public. This is an important lesson I learned early in my campaign. Those who stand up and speak out are the true leaders in our communities, and you can be one of those people. There truthfully is no reason why you cannot. It takes courage and commitment. **Age is NOT a prerequisite to be a leader in your community. Never forget that.**

While I am unique for being the youngest elected official ever in Syosset, New York, candidates from across the United States have also chosen to run for and have successfully held office at a young age. Though they each were similar in age demographic, these young candidates sought elected office for a myriad of reasons.

For Connor Kurtz, a resident of Amity Township in Pennsylvania and a current senior at The Catholic University of America, a daily drive through his neighborhood where he passed by his district's middle school prompted him to eventually run for his local school board. Connor recalls driving by his town's middle school, which was a relatively new building, as a 17-year-old student in the Daniel Boone Area School District in Pennsylvania. Connor says he, "Noticed that the American flag was way too small to be flying on the flagpole. It was shredded, torn and faded, and the

Pennsylvania flag was in even worse condition." Connor questioned how, "...you have administrators who drive by, students go by, parents, and members of the community; has nobody thought to replace it? **If no one noticed that, what else are people missing?"** Connor went to his board of education's monthly meeting, where he noticed two "huge flat screen televisions in the cafeteria." He was puzzled how the district "had money for televisions in the cafeteria but no money for a new American Flag?" When Connor addressed the dilapidated state of the American Flag at the middle school, he was met with a warm reception, "the audience interrupted me with applause," he recollects. He kept going back, as he, "Wanted to hear about how other items were being brought up, and what new business was being resolved. As somebody who will pay taxes, I want to know how the money is being spent." When it came time for the school board elections, he thought it would be really interesting to run, but he "never anticipated being elected." Not only was Connor elected, but he won with major numbers; he won both the Republican and Democratic primaries by double digits (in some states, like Pennsylvania, school board elections are partisan, and in others, like New York, they are non-partisan) and was soundly elected at the age of 18 in the 2011 general election as the nominee for both major parties. As this book was being written, Connor, now 22 years old, had just won both the Republican and Democratic nominations for re-election to the Daniel Boone Area Board of School Directors.

As I mentioned in the acknowledgements, Tom DiNapoli has been a mentor of mine ever since I was a teenager. I'll always remember how Tom took time out of his day, as he does for so many young candidates, to meet me back in 2011 when I first began campaigning.

To this day he coaches me on all things political, focusing on **the difference between being a politician and a public servant—a dichotomy he never lets me forget.**

At 61 years old, Tom DiNapoli was re-elected to his third term as New York State Comptroller in November 2014 with over 60% of the vote and 2,233,057 votes statewide.[15] For those not familiar with his position, the New York State Comptroller is the "state's chief fiscal officer who ensures that state and local governments use taxpayer money effectively and efficiently to promote the common good," and is the "sole trustee of the $184.5 billion New York State Common Retirement Fund."[16]

However Tom DiNapoli is no political neophyte; his career in politics began when he became the first 18-year-old elected to public office in the history of New York State, winning election to the Mineola School Board of Education on Long Island in 1972.[17]

Let's put this in historical context; when Tom ran for the school board, 18 year olds had just gotten the right to vote! Yes, just one year prior in 1971, the 26th amendment was ratified, lowering the voting age from 21 to 18.[18]

Tom, then president of his senior class at Mineola High School, ran for the school board because he was concerned about policies and practices. He was

---

[15] "Thomas DiNapoli - Ballotpedia." 2013. 20 Oct. 2015 <http://ballotpedia.org/Thomas_DiNapoli>
[16] "Office of the New York State Comptroller - About the ..." 20 Oct. 2015 <http://www.osc.state.ny.us/about/response.htm>
[17] "About Comptroller DiNapoli - Office of the New York State ..." 20 Oct. 2015 <http://www.osc.state.ny.us/about/bio.htm>
[18] "The 26th Amendment - Democracy Day." 2011. 20 Oct. 2015 <http://democracyday.com/the-26th-amendment.html>

a frequent attendee at school board meetings, where he would often step up to the microphone and express his opinions to the board members sitting at the dais regarding issues facing the district. He recalls how, "A lot of the incumbents felt like the 'old guard.'" One meeting, before he announced his candidacy, there was a district-wide committee established to evaluate curriculum. Tom discussed how, "The Mineola Board of Education was bragging about how inclusive it was, with representatives from the Chamber of Commerce, various community groups...but there were no students on the committee!" When Tom asked why there were no students on the committee, the answer he got from the board was short and honest; they "just didn't think to include students."

With such a dismissive answer, Tom felt that he didn't want the students to be left out any longer. "It made me think that we have to shake things up," Tom says. He theorized that because, "Voter turnout is low, and there is often no contest for incumbents, **by my running I was going to ensure that we're [students] not overlooked anymore.**"

The slightest event, or an occurrence in everyday life, can trigger a life of public service.

Just as Connor Kurtz was inspired to run for office from a routine drive, Tom decided to seek elected office from an answer he received at one of the many board of education meetings he attended.

If the Mineola School Board had included student representatives on the curriculum committee, maybe he wouldn't have run for office. If the district had replaced the flag at the middle school, maybe Connor would have chosen to forego a run for his school board.

You see, many people who wind up running for office pursue it because of something that happens to them during everyday life. Whether you run because you received your property tax bill and were appalled with the percentage increase, or you were at the park and felt the town wasn't properly maintaining public spaces, or you were at a town hall and thought the agenda was not transparent enough, our government is *supposed* to be made up of citizens who want to effect change in their communities (I use the word *supposed* because clearly this is not the case at all levels of government, i.e. the United States Congress). That's why when young people write off the possibility of ever running for elected office, I tell them to heed John Lennon's advice when he said that, "Life is what happens while you are busy making other plans."[19]

Take West Virginia's Saira Blair. Saira, whose father Craig Blair is a State Senator in West Virginia, says that she, "First got interested in politics at the age of 6 when my dad ran for the House of Delegates." She remembers how she helped out on his campaigns, but she confesses that, **"I never thought I would do it [run for office] myself at a young age...I thought I could only run at 40 or 50."** Just like Connor and Tom, she would seek elected office because of an event in her life. For Saira, now a sophomore at West Virginia University, this event was West Virginia's *Youth in Government* program. Saira recalls how at 16, "I participated in *Youth in Government*, where 300 high school students went to West Virginia's Capitol, wrote pieces of legislation, and presented them on the house floor, getting the true experience of serving in the legislature." According to Saira, this weekend,

---

[19] "Life is what happens while you are busy making other plans ..." 2003. 20 Oct. 2015
<http://www.brainyquote.com/quotes/quotes/j/johnlennon137162.htm l>

"Changed my life...it showed I could have an impact when I saw just how amazing the other students were." Saira notes that, "West Virginia is the only state with a declining population and battles with Arkansas and Mississippi for lowest net income per capita." It's these statistics, and this grim reality for West Virginians that motivates Saira as a delegate to find solutions, "To keep students here in West Virginia."

Let's head west to Seattle, and meet my good friend Cyrus Habib.

For Cyrus Habib, early adversity in his life set the stage for his eventual ascension to Washington State's Senate. Cyrus, the first Iranian American ever elected to a state legislature, lost his eyesight early in life due to illness.[20] He says that, "Having become blind at age eight due to cancer, I have this experience of having benefited from public schools, social services, and state support. **If you give every kid opportunities equal or better to what I had, you're going to see remarkable income growth, opportunity growth, and a reduction in the need for social services."**

There were a multitude of other factors involved in Cyrus' rise to prominence in Washington State's Senate. After growing up in the area he currently represents, he left the state for higher education, receiving a BA from Columbia University and a JD from Yale Law School. Cyrus says that after finishing law school, "I was faced with the choice of doing what many of my classmates were doing and practicing law in New York, DC, and San Francisco, or coming back to my

---

[20] "Cyrus Habib: The first Iranian American ever elected to state ..." 2012. 20 Oct. 2015 <http://features.kodoom.com/en/iranian-diaspora/cyrus-habib-the-first-iranian-american-ever-elected-to-state-legislature/v/4766/>

hometown." Cyrus opted to move back to Seattle where his introduction to politics came when his mother ran unsuccessfully for a seat on the Superior Court in 2008. Cyrus recalls getting to know both Seattle's political environment from his mother's campaign, and the professional environment from working during summers at the Perkins Coie law firm. He found that, "I like this political environment that's progressive and accessible, and I like that the [law] firm is supportive of my being involved in the community."

Living in the "techy suburbs" of Seattle, with an "increasingly young, very diverse population with a good number of Millennials," he discovered the political culture to be, "Rigid in old, suburban legacy." He says, "As I became active in rotary, chamber, non-profit work, there were not that many people with a younger Millennial perspective in government." Moreover, as someone working with start-ups in the technology sector, he says that there was, "No legislator in Olympia working on entrepreneurial issues...so when there was a seat open in the State House because of a retirement, I decided to run for it." Cyrus was elected at 31 to Washington State's House, and two years later to its State Senate.

As this book is being written, Cyrus, now 34, has announced his campaign for Lieutenant Governor of Washington! In an interview with the Seattle Times, Cyrus proudly claims that, "I'm passionate about big-picture issues of justice, but also how can the law be used as a tool kit to get where we need to go."[21]

---

[21] "State Sen. Cyrus Habib to run for lieutenant governor | The ..." 2015. 20 Oct. 2015 <http://www.seattletimes.com/seattle-news/politics/state-sen-cyrus-habib-to-run-for-lieutenant-governor/>

Overcoming adversity is a common thread among the young elected officials in this book. Anthony Fasano was no different; he was a major underdog in his race.

Anthony Fasano is from Hopatcong, a New Jersey town an hour west of New York City. Anthony, who like Tom DiNapoli was also president of his senior class at Hopatcong High School, became one of the youngest elected officials in New Jersey at age 19. Anthony claims that, "It was my involvement in student government in middle school and high school, and realizing that there might be a disconnect between students and the administration and the board of education that made me want to run for the school board." Anthony discussed the major issues facing Hopatcong Schools and his community, most notably that, "Students and parents didn't believe in the district...hundreds of students would leave the district to get their education somewhere else." In addition, the district was facing, "Major financial woes, the curriculum wasn't updated...policy and board-wise we failed to see" the issues at hand. Anthony has a great passion for his community, and thought, **"Who better to fix the situation than me?"** As a student, he had a front-row seat to the issues that needed to be addressed. Moreover, Anthony felt his experience in student government prepared him to serve on the board, "Organizing class trips, fundraisers, prom, coordinating efforts with the board of education...it made me realize I could do what they do and I could do a better job of it." Anthony maintains that this "is still my attitude now."

Flash forward to present day and Anthony, also a student trustee at Montclair University in New Jersey, is vice president of the Hopatcong Board of Education after being elected by his colleagues.

Unfortunately not all of the elected officials I reached out to for this book agreed to be interviewed. Of those who said no, the majority were already established in their careers. While certainly discouraging, what reinvigorated me were the conversations I had with seasoned veterans of politics like Marcus Molinaro, who spent a great deal of time on the phone with me answering each and every question I peppered him with.

When I asked Marcus Molinaro, current Dutchess County Executive in upstate New York, why he ran for Mayor of Tivoli at age 19 in 1995, he responded that, "A better question is what made me run for village trustee the year before." In 1994 Marcus had just graduated high school, and was interning for New York State Assemblywoman Eileen Hickey. He says that, "I always liked government, politics, and public service...I always had an interest in national politics, **but I never really paid attention to local politics...that's where the action is, and it's what impacts your life.**" He continues that he started to attend village board meetings, where, "People were looking to improve services." Tivoli was not thriving economically, "With vacant buildings, old parks...people were looking for a sense of enthusiasm and energy." Tivoli was a small town of about 1,300 residents. Marcus was "working at a local pizza place," which gave him the opportunity to "meet everybody." He remembers that he decided to "give this a try." He ran for one of the two village trustee seats in a four-person race. Marcus was elected that year with the most votes of any candidate in the race. He jokes that the next year, when the incumbent mayor for 20 years asked if any of the incumbent board members wanted to succeed him, he ran home and asked his mom! I assume his mother said yes. In March of 1995, he ran successfully in an unopposed race and became mayor.

This May, Marcus announced his bid for a second term as Dutchess County Executive. *The Poughkeepsie Journal*, a local news site covering the town of Poughkeepsie in Dutchess County, wrote that Marcus, "Citing Dutchess County's 'strong financial position and return to fiscal stability'...said in a news release that the county is 'ready for a comeback.'"[22] I'm thrilled to report that as this book was being written, voters returned Marc for a second term.

Finding young elected officials to be interviewed for this book was a challenge in itself. As mentioned previously, when I was first running there were no publications or books available specifically concerning the area of youths running for office; I had to Google search "18 year old runs for school board." So I searched similar phrases such as "teenager elected" and "young people in government." I'm so grateful that my research led me to Ellen Nesbitt.

For Ellen Nesbitt, politics just ran in the family. Ellen, elected to the Dutchess County Legislator in New York at 19 in 2013, had a pretty good political advisor at her disposal; her father had served as a Dutchess County, New York Legislator a decade before she ran. Ellen recalls how, "I used to go campaigning with my dad and my youngest sister" (Ellen laughs as she remembers that her dad had to bribe her younger sister to go). She jokes that while, "She [her younger sister] hated it, I loved it." Even as a nine year old, Ellen used to tell her father that, "I want to do the talking." Her pitch was short and sweet. "Hey my name's Ellen, my

---

[22] "Molinaro announces re-election bid." 2015. 20 Oct. 2015 <http://www.poughkeepsiejournal.com/story/news/local/2015/05/06/molinaro-announces-re-election-bid/70889232/>

dad's running for county legislator, please vote for him," she recalls. Ellen now teasingly admits, "That was really obnoxious for a 9 year old," but she noted that, "I got my spiel down." Ironically, when Marcus Molinaro was elected mayor of Tivoli, NY, at the age of 19, Ellen went to see him speak. She felt it, "Was really exciting...he accomplished so much at a young age...I knew there was an open seat [on the County Legislature], so I talked to my dad and said, 'what if I ran?'" **She felt that residents weren't being represented the way that they should be, and felt that she could do a better job.** Clearly, the voters agreed. As this book was being written, Ellen was just re-elected to her seat in the Dutchess County Legislature.

Let's jump back to my beloved Long Island, where we'll meet a hometown hero, Michaelle Solages.

Michaelle Solages, a Long Island native, has a special place in this book; she is the only candidate that I've had the privilege of campaigning with. In the days after Hurricane Sandy, Michaelle, her brother Carrie, who himself was elected at 32 to the Nassau County Legislature in November of 2011, and I set out to make sure residents had important information about emergency contacts, shelters, and FEMA reimbursement programs.[23] Standing in front of the Western Beef Supermarket in Roosevelt, New York (a 20-minute drive east from JFK airport), shaking hands with residents and reminding them to stay safe, the reception from voters was incredible. In fact, Michaelle caught national notoriety that week, with the LA Times inking a story with the title "New York Assembly

---

[23] "Ciotti, Solages face off in 3rd Legislative District – LI Herald ..." 2014. 20 Oct. 2015 <http://liherald.com/stories/Ciotti-Solages-face-off-in-3rd-Legislative-District,36009?page=2&content_source=>

Candidate Campaigns in Sandy's Gas Lines." As the article notes, "She [Michaelle] carries a notepad that is filling up with the addresses of those she meets whose homes still lack power...calling the Long Island Power Authority to relay where the lines need to be restored."[24]

Michaelle was elected in 2012 at the age of 27 to the New York State Assembly. Graduating from Hofstra University on Long Island in 2007, Michaelle was keenly aware of the issues in both her community and statewide. She says that, **"Currently Millennials exceed Baby Boomers in population, and while there's a lot of conversation in government geared towards seniors and adults...Millennials are not being addressed...I wanted to make a change in my community."** Michaelle wanted to, "Expand small businesses, help young families and new workers. I graduated during the Great Recession, and many of my classmates who graduated left with zero career opportunities." She recalls how it was "all of these problems that inspired me to run for office." Due to redistricting in New York, the 22nd Assembly District was created, which Michaelle says, "Gave me the opportunity to run." With "everybody leaving Long Island, even businesses leaving," Michaelle knew it was her time to step up and serve. Michaelle, now 30 and serving her second term in the New York State Assembly, was nominated this year for the EMILY's List Gabrielle Giffords Rising Star Award, honoring "extraordinary women in state or local office."

Many of the young elected officials interviewed for this book come from political families. Saira Blair's

---

[24] "New York Assembly candidate campaigns in Sandy's gas ..." 2012. 20 Oct. 2015 <http://articles.latimes.com/2012/nov/04/nation/la-na-nn-sandy-ny-gas-lines-20121104>

father is a state senator. Ellen Nesbitt's dad is a county legislator, as is Michaelle Solage's brother. And Cyrus Habib's mom sought a seat on the bench of the Superior Court. The same rings true for Ian Calderon who says that, "Public service has been in my family since I was born."

In 2012, at 27 years old, Ian was elected to the California State Assembly, becoming the youngest legislator in the state.[25] His father Charles was not only the "first Latino attorney ever elected to the California State Senate," but the first person in California's history to have served as the majority leader in both the California Assembly and California Senate. Ian says that he spoke to his father about the possibility of running for office, but his knowledge of elective office actually made him hesitant about pursuing it. Ian says that, "For me, it's what my dad did...I had so much love and respect for people in elective office because of him...but I knew the difficulties of the job, and I knew the job was so important that there was a lingering thought in me that there was no way I could do this." Ian equated this doubt about how we perceive our parents as "superheroes," and often have a tough time believing we can do what they do. He says, "The fact that I was young, it was something I struggled with." It's important to stop and emphasize this—if you're thinking about running and are having second thoughts; if you are in the midst of your campaign and are feeling down; if you are contemplating a rematch from your last race and are nervous, do you know what that makes you? Completely normal. I slept a grand total of 15 hours in the week preceding my election.

---

[25] "Bio - Ian Calderon." 2014. 20 Oct. 2015
<http://www.ianccalderon.com/about-ian>

Politics is emotional. You're allowed to feel uneasy at times. Just don't let that doubt, or those nerves, hold you back from chasing your dream.

Ian was actually a decorated surfer growing up in Los Angeles County, with surf apparel giant Hurley International as his main sponsor. He later took a job with Hurley as a retail marketing manager. After two years with Hurley, he found that this was not his passion. He proceeded to have more conversations with his father about running for office. Before the Passage of Proposition 28, reducing the term limits to a total of 12 years in both state houses, legislators could serve 6 years in the State Assembly and 8 years in the State Senate, and, "My father was going to be terming out."[26] After taking a job with California Assemblyman Ed Hernandez, Ian says that he had what he calls his "ah hah" moment; the moment where he knew that politics was what he should be doing with his life. Ian recalls that, "within my first week, I was doing constituent case work. There was a single mother who called in because she was having an issue with receiving unemployment benefits." He continues, "Every time this woman spoke to the person she needed, the line would go dead, or they would hang up on her. This was a several month process for her, yet within a week I was able to help secure her unemployment benefits." This of course was a job well done by Ian, but the "ah hah" moment came when the woman "called me afterwards and told me 'I can't tell you how much your help means to me...I don't want to be accepting unemployment, I want a job.'" Ian says that, **"For me to know I did something to**

---

[26] "California Term Limits | League of Women Voters of California." 2014. 24 Oct. 2015 <https://lwvc.org/issues/california-term-limits>

help someone else, when you find what you're supposed to do in life you have an 'ah hah' moment, and this was my 'ah hah' moment."

This phenomenon of the "ah hah" moment happens to many people in different times throughout their lives. However, few have the bravery to act upon it, showcasing the true courage of their convictions. Ian Calderon found what he was meant to do, and acted upon it. Ian, now 30 and serving his second term, is the chairman of the Assembly's Committee on Arts, Entertainment, Sports, Tourism, and Internet Media.[27]

For Maine's Justin Chenette, now 24 years old, he humorously contends that his eventual ascent to elected office is because "he couldn't keep his mouth shut." Justin announced his candidacy for State Representative for the City of Saco while he was a junior at Linden State College in Vermont in December of 2011. He says that he decided to run out of frustration; he was "never somebody who always wanted to run for office, never a political science major." He was simply a student who wanted to be a reporter. However, it became hard for Justin to pursue reporting, noting that there is, "Too much of a barrier as a journalist where I could not take action. I could report, but I couldn't fulfill my civic duty because of a professional barrier." Justin continues that, **"If you're passionate about something but you can't fight for what you believe because of your job, ultimately I started to realize this might become an issue later."** Justin summarily filed the paperwork to run, "Without even talking to my party or talking to the incumbent." His decision paid off, and in 2012,

---

[27] "Bio - Ian Calderon." 2014. 24 Oct. 2015
<http://www.ianccalderon.com/about-ian>

Justin was elected at age 21, becoming the youngest legislator in the state of Maine.

Justin is a great example of a person who possesses a crucial character trait for serving in elected office-communication. Now, of course you don't have to earn a BS in Broadcast News like Justin to be effective in office. But communication is key; whether it's a speech, a press conference, a written press release, a debate or any of the various activities politicians participate in, communication is a vital skill. **Joining the speech and debate team is a great way to improve your communication skills.** Having been a state finalist in extemporaneous speech and a national finalist in congressional debate, I credit the speech and debate team for fostering my ability to formulate solid arguments, speak in front of large groups, and write coherent policy positions.

Let's now meet my favorite Staten Islander, the one and only Nicole Malliotakis.

For Nicole, it was after she earned an insider's perspective into the workings of New York State's government did she decide to seek a bid to the NYS Assembly. Nicole was appointed by then Governor George Pataki to be a liaison for her home of Staten Island and parts of New York City. Working for the New York governor was her first job in politics, and "an opportunity to meet a lot of people and network." After working at Con Edison as a public affairs manager, Nicole became even more cognizant of the breadth of issues facing the working class.[28] Nicole recalls that, "Commuting from Manhattan, I was not happy about tolls rising, bus fares rising...I felt it was crazy to shell

[28] "Nicole Malliotakis - New York State Assembly Home." 2011. 24 Oct. 2015 <http://assembly.state.ny.us/mem/Nicole-Malliotakis/bio/>

out more money for less service." Moreover, "Albany hadn't passed a budget and it was August, which would make that year's budget the latest budget (passed) in the history of New York...it was simply dysfunctional." Nicole realized it was incumbent upon her to step up and run; she felt that, **"This is my generation who is inheriting this debt, we are the ones affected by these policies."** Though she ran against a four-year incumbent, and admits she was considered a long shot, she says that, "We had the right message." This message resonated with voters, as Nicole would prevail by 10 percentage points on Election Day.[29]

Let's cross over the Hudson River into New Jersey, where we'll meet Chase Harrison.

For Chase Harrison, a combination of political aspiration and a concern over student-life issues led him to a candidacy for a seat on the Millburn School Board of Education in New Jersey. Chase says that:

> "I have had an interest in politics for the majority of my life...when I realized that I would be eligible, I figured simply running would be a phenomenal way to gain experience in campaigning. I've worked on senatorial and congressional campaigns before but being the candidate is a completely different experience. If I won (which I didn't think would happen), **I knew serving as a board of education member would be incredible and allow me to learn so much about public service, finance, management, etc."**

---

[29] "Nicole Malliotakis, an upstart from Rosebank, runs ..." 2010. 24 Oct. 2015
<http://www.silive.com/news/index.ssf/2010/11/nicole_malliotakis_an_upstart.html>

Chase does state, however, that, "The more prominent reason I ran was because I felt that student life issues in Millburn weren't being addressed nearly to the level they required." Millburn High School is one of New Jersey's highest performing public school districts, and as Chase believes, "Expects its student to perform at an extremely high level." As a student, Chase recalls that, "While having rigorous schools should be the aim of any district...I recognized that the expectations on Millburn students were creating intense negative effects on student mental health and student well-being." He continued that, "I felt Millburn needed an advocate on behalf of students who could dedicate himself to coming up with concrete solutions to these problems." Chase successfully won a seat on the Millburn Board of Education in 2013, and after enrolling in Sarah Lawrence College he transferred to the University of Chicago in the fall of 2015. Chase hits an important point; without a voice to speak for them, the youth get ignored. **There is *no one* lobbying for our youth. Therefore, I believe we must begin to represent ourselves, since clearly no one will be doing it for us. It's time that youth becomes a formidable presence in politics no different than seniors, veterans, and religious groups.**

There must be something in the water in New Jersey; Brandon Pugh, our next elected official, also calls the Garden State home.

For Brandon Pugh, similar to Chase Harrison, he also attended a high-performing high school in Moorestown, New Jersey. Brandon, elected to the Moorestown Board of Education at 19 and now the fourth most senior member on his board of education only three years later, says that, "I wanted to make sure that what I received in high school continued. We have a high-performing school district and I wanted to make sure it remained." Brandon holds that his experience as a student, coupled with his youth, are vital assets to his ability to serve on the board of education. He says that, **"All Board of Education members came from the same background, had the same experiences...nobody that was actually [a student] in the district, or closely removed from the district, was on the board."** Brandon uniquely describes this as using a "customer perspective," allowing him to, "Make decisions because I often have a different perspective...it makes for a more diverse board" in terms of thought, practice, and style. In addition to his election to his school board, at 21, Brandon was elected as president of the Burlington County School Boards' Association in New Jersey.

Specifically when it comes to school boards, between my own board and board members from neighboring towns, the stories of why adult residents ran for a seat in the first place are pretty similar. Residents got involved with the PTA and wanted to increase their involvement in the district. Parents were concerned with curriculum (i.e. the Common Core Standards) and wanted to oversee its changes and implementation. Residents were unhappy with the tax rate that year and wanted to see where all of the money was going.

While important, and these are all issues I pay major attention to, I find these stories stale. Where is the zeal to protect school district prestige the way Brandon had felt? Where is the urgency to be a voice for students like Chase felt? Where is the motivation to reform education and bring it into the 21st century like I strive to do? **This is a major reason why I wrote this book; the narratives told by many adult candidates are tired, and the stories young**

people want to tell are inspiring. First-time candidates teeming with fresh, altruistic intentions, new ideas that actually serve *real* students, and the general public, can win. It's time they run.

Lack of age diversity was a major concern for numerous candidates in this book, including Doug Pascarella. I met Doug when I worked for the Nassau County Executive's Office in the summer of 2011, and he was an incredible resource for me during my candidacy for the Syosset School Board.

For Doug, the absence of age diversity on his town's board of education was a driving factor in his 2004 candidacy for the Plainedge School Board on Long Island, New York. Doug was class president at the time of his election and was, "Very interested in politics and the student council in high school. I was very curious about the board of education as it's what affects you as a high school student." Doug explains the board at that time, "Was comprised of middle-aged moms and dads in the 40-50 age range. It simply was not diverse enough, and diversity was needed." Additionally, **"All but one of the school board members didn't even graduate from Plainedge. They don't have an accurate sense of what the school district is like."** Doug would win his election, and at age 18, became one of the youngest elected officials in New York. Doug, now 29, is an Assistant to Long Island, New York's Nassau County Executive Ed Mangano.

As Long Islanders, aside from Ralph's Italian Ices and Little Vincent's Pizza, we love our beaches. Let's head west to a place where it's closer to drive to Canada than a beach, and meet my favorite Montanan, Daniel Zolnikov.

For Daniel Zolnikov, he was a University of Montana graduate who says he was tired of Montana politicians occupying an office and not having the courage of their convictions. Daniel was elected to the Montana House of Representatives at 25. He contends that, **"Politicians have no spine. I wanted to be a guy who actually stood for causes."** Daniel continues that, "People worry about what they do next in politics...I wanted to remove that self-preservation aspect and actually stand for something, so at least I got into politics right for the right reasons." Daniel recalls that he made it a priority to get to know those who were politically involved at the beginning of his exploration of a candidacy. He claims that after speaking with them, "We found we were pretty like minded in some areas." As the Republican Party was looking for candidates, they "asked me to run for a seat." Not only would he eventually win that seat, but he would win re-election two years later in 2014. Daniel admits that he, "Knew nothing about campaigning, knew nothing about raising money, didn't know how any of it worked, and the issues were new to me." But, he was not afraid to speak his mind, and share what he believed it. Montana voters rewarded that, and made him one of the youngest elected officials in the state.

      I want to emphasize Daniel's point regarding the aspect of "self-preservation" in politics, and the notion that politicians will do anything and say anything to stay in office. What this means is that these career politician-types are inauthentic, untruthful, and flip-flop on issues.

      This is what makes you different.

      It's this fearlessness, this desire to serve not because you want to stay in office and collect a paycheck, but because you want to effect positive change in your community that can be an x-factor in your election. It's not an accident that candidates who have a virtual impossibility of being elected president are the ones who speak the truth most often. Elise Stefanik, the youngest woman ever elected to Congress, embraced this exact mentality. She recalls how, "Every expert told me, 'You're not going to win,' [so] willingness to lose was important."[30]

      If you are sincere, voters will see it; genuine intentions cannot be faked.

      From mountains and cattle ranches, let's head back to the Eastern Seaboard where we meet Daniel Croson from New Jersey.

      For Daniel Croson, a board of education trustee from Carteret, New Jersey, working in politics gave him an introduction into what holding elected office looks like. Daniel says he sought elected office because he was, "Always involved in politics, and I wanted to see change in my community." Before seeking office himself, Daniel worked for several other candidates he believed in, like current Carteret Mayor Daniel Reiman. He recalls how he, "Worked very hard to see good people in office who cared about what I care about." However, it occurred to Daniel that, **"What better way to effect change than by doing it directly rather than indirectly?"** Daniel continues, "I spent years talking to voters on behalf of other candidates," including serving as the political director for the Mayor of Carteret from 2010-2013. This experience helped him run a successful campaign in November of 2013. At 22 he was elected to the Carteret Board of Education in New Jersey, becoming one of the youngest elected officials in the state.

---

[30] "New York Representative Elise Stefanik: I was … - Fortune." 2015. 24 Oct. 2015 <http://fortune.com/2015/10/12/representative-stefanik-new-york/>

Let's head to warmer weather, and meet Das
Williams on the west coast.

For Das Williams, a current California
Assemblymember from Santa Barbara, California,
economic circumstances prompted his eventual
candidacy for the California State Assembly. First
elected to the Santa Barbara City Council at 28, Das
claims that, "I decided to run for the [California] State
Assembly in 2009, when we were still suffering from
the worst of the Great Recession. I saw this challenge as
a calling for me to run for state office and to do my part
to get our state back on track." As the California
Assembly's 37th district representative, he continues
that, **"California's values were being deeply
eroded due to the terrible economic crisis and
I'm glad to say that, after four years in office,
we've been able to reinvest in our education
system, stand up for the rights of working
families, and pass some of the strongest
environmental protections in the nation."**

From LAX to JFK, we're back in the Empire
State to meet Jon Fiore.

For Jon Fiore, a controversy in his "very small
and closely-knit" New York Mills community would
serve as a precursor to his run for the New York Mills
Union Free School District Board of Education in May
of 2014. Jon explains the situation in his upstate New
York hometown thoroughly below:

"The only tension within the community was
regarding the basketball coach, Mr. Michael Adey.
[July of 2013] bore witness to one of the most
highly-attended board meetings in school history,
as the board had to consider whether or not to
rehire the coach. To give some backstory, Coach
Adey is now the winningest coach in Section III

history, and is a member of the New York State Basketball Hall of Fame. The source of the tension could be traced back to two issues: Coach Adey had kept relatively poor records of equipment and funding for the team...and the other issue being that he had a tendency to give very little playing time to non-starters on the team. Being that I was a manager on the basketball team, a large number of community members asked how I felt about my coach, and I always would tell them that the man has a heart of gold and he did his very best to help make the team not only better basketball players, but better men in general.

[July's Board meeting] was the first board meeting that I had ever attended. During the public comment session, I spoke on behalf of my coach and said that if the board failed to act in a manner that the public wanted, I would either help any candidate that decided to run against any sitting board member who refused to represent their constituents' views or even run myself when the time came. After the board reluctantly voted to approve the personnel report...I began to pay attention to the affairs of the Board with an eye for detail.

Then in the midst of my senior year, the superintendent, whom I had always been close with because she was my elementary principal until I went on to middle school, at which point she also became the superintendent, jokingly suggested I run for one of the two soon to be vacant seats on the board. I gave the matter a great deal of thought, and I decided I was going to run."

Jon states that voters were certainly not expecting him to run for the board. "I was greeted with surprise and shock at first," he recalls. However, Jon remembers that this initial shock turned into encouragement after voters began to consider him as a serious contender for the board. Jon says that this surprise, **"Quickly turned to support and enthusiasm as I proved myself to be a viable candidate on each and every doorstep that gave me the opportunity."** After being elected in 2014, Jon is currently studying accounting at Utica College in New York.

Though different in nature, just as there was controversy in Jon Fiore's hometown, a "major political scandal" in Hamilton Township, New Jersey, home of Chris Scales, served as a backdrop for his campaign. Chris describes the scandal below, which involved, "the town mayor and allegedly, school board members."

> "The insurance broker was a friend of my town's mayor and school board officials, funneling thousands of dollars to them via straw donations and gifts. With a bribe of $12,400, the insurance broker attempted to use the mayor's influence to persuade two board of education members to not put her contract out for bid. The mayor was charged with extortion, bribery, and money laundering, sending him to prison on a 24-month sentence. The school board officials who the insurance broker allegedly donated money to their campaign and hoped to have the mayor use his influence on, have not been charged with any wrongdoing. None of these board members are serving currently."

Chris served as a non-voting member of the Hamilton Township Board of Education for three years from 2011-2014. He states that, "He was there when those two major events took place." Speaking to his duties as a non-voting member, Chris details that, "The role of a non-voting member on a school board is to report to the Board about things taking place at your respective High School." Chris remembers his time as a new representative fondly, saying how he would be, "Eagerly waiting until the next board meeting. I took pride in my position, enjoyed meeting the 'regulars' that come to the meetings, and working one-on-one with my principal." **However, this fondness grew into frustration during his second and third year as a representative. He believes that this stemmed from, "The decisions being made by the board, the lack of transparency, public trust, and maturity displayed by some members."** Fondness turned into frustration, frustration turned into action, and action turned into success; in 2014, as an 18-year - old freshman at Rider University Lawrence Township, New Jersey, Chris Scales was elected to the Hamilton Township District Board of Education.

In contrast to Jon Fiore and Chris Scales, controversy was non-existent in Mark Kremer's hometown of Southgate, Michigan. When asked about the existence of community unrest towards the district, Mark answered that, "There was not tension between the community and elected officials to my knowledge...we have good people in the Southgate City government." Mark says that, **"I have always wanted to give back to the community. I have always wanted to get involved in politics and elective government. I want to make a difference, and I saw my opportunity to do so. I took that opportunity, and I got it."** Like Chris Scales, Mark was the student government representative from his high school to the board of education, and this familiarity with the district led him to feel a bit like an "insider." However, Mark says that, "In a way I was an outsider as well. I had never been elected to local, state, or federal government before as I was only 18." This mixture of his knowledge of the district's workings, and his ability to bring a fresh perspective to the table was a winning combination; as an 18-year-old student at Asher Alternative High School Southgate, Michigan, he was elected in November of 2014 as the youngest trustee ever to join the Southgate Community Schools Board of Education.[31]

---

[31] "Youngest Southgate school board member looks forward to ..." 2015. 24 Oct. 2015
<http://thenewsherald.com/articles/2015/01/06/news/doc54a6bc7c3a0 6c037947811.txt>

<u>Tips</u>

#1 Running for class president is a great segue into politics. A great deal of the young elected officials in this book who were presidents of their classes went on to successfully win seats on their respective boards of education.

#2 Find out whether the office you are running for is partisan or non-partisan. If it's non-partisan, like school board elections in New York, it may be wise to remain an independent, therefore appealing to voters of both major parties. If it's partisan, like school board elections in Pennsylvania, heed Daniel Zolnikov's advice and meet the involved members of the party and see how they feel about issues of importance to you.

#3 If you are running because you simply want to pursue a career in politics, be honest about it! Voters appreciate genuine candidates, and will see right through insincere motives.

#4 If you know which elected office you seek, go to as many public meetings of that governing body as you can. You will learn a great deal about how that organization operates by observation, and voters will undoubtedly ask you if you've been to a meeting.

#5 Joining the speech and debate team is a great way to improve your communication skills. Having been a state finalist in extemporaneous speech and a national finalist in congressional debate, I credit the speech and debate team for fostering my ability to formulate solid arguments, speak in front of large groups, and write coherent policy positions.

Chapter Summary

- **Running for office is hard.** Holding elected office is often harder. As Assemblymember Nicole Malliotakis said earlier, you, "Really have to want to do this...you have to have a passion or you won't do a good job."
- **Don't sell out!** Many believe that the end justifies the means in campaigns, and that a candidate must win at all costs. Sacrificing your principles, or taking the easy way out, is not worth getting elected. Win or lose, finish your race with the same integrity that you began it with.
- **People run for office for a myriad of reasons**; there is no right or wrong answer for why you seek elected office, and do not let anybody tell you otherwise. Seeking elected office is a right that every citizen in this country has once they turn 18; even though a candidate may be older by several years or decades, they are no more entitled to that office than you are.
- **Many will complain in private, but few will speak up in public**. Those who do stand up and speak out are the true leaders in our communities, and there is no reason that you cannot be one. It takes courage, and it takes commitment, but age is NOT a prerequisite to be a leader in your community. Never forget that.
- **Use the elected officials in this book as a resource.** Those interviewed in this book were able to navigate the treacherous terrain that is a campaign and emerge victorious. They all agreed to be interviewed because they realize the need for more young people to run for office. Please do not hesitate to reach out to those in this book for guidance. Additionally, if you live near one of the elected officials ask to volunteer on a re-election campaign or serve as a committee volunteer.

We are the Millennial generation, and when one of us succeeds, we all succeed.

A Difficult Endeavor

So you've decided to step up and run for a public office. Congratulations. That decision is tough, gutsy, and noble; I promise that it will ultimately be worthwhile and change your life.

I feel it's crucial, however, that I impress upon you in this chapter, a very important lesson this book aims to teach; running for office at a young age is an incredibly difficult undertaking.

A great deal of this difficulty stems from handling the criticism and doubt of others. Justin Chenette of Saco, Maine, says that the presence of skepticism made his campaign difficult, with an undertone of "can he really do this?" following him everywhere he went as he campaigned. Justin, like many interviewed in this book, says that this question surrounding his seriousness as a candidate still lingers. He jokes that the skepticism even included observations about his appearance, such as "you have spiky hair, and you look really young." He notes that while there was precedence of a 21 year old running for office in his community, it was "a long time ago." Justin believes that he couldn't have navigated the degree of difficulty that comes with running for office at a young age without his mentor, Linda Valentino. Linda Valentino was the incumbent representative from Maine's 15th district, serving Justin's hometown of Saco, who he was running to succeed as she ran for Maine's State Senate that year. He says that Valentino endorsed him, and was his "mentor" who "helped me through the process. I probably wouldn't have been State Representative without her." Thanks to the help of now-State Senator Valentino, **Justin is setting a new precedent for**

young elected officials in Maine as the United States' youngest openly LGBT legislator.[32]

As mentioned in the introduction, young candidates are almost always surrounded by an immense cloud of doubt over whether they can actually win a race. I remember how hurt I felt when, after excitedly telling an officer of Syosset, Long Island's PTA how I would seek a seat on the board the following May, I was met with the remark that, **"Nobody is going to vote for an 18 year old," and that, "I had no chance of winning."** Though this definitely offended me, I was able to eventually brush it off as a classic case of an adult telling a kid they couldn't do something. However, when I received even worse skepticism from kids my own age, I truly was rattled. I will never forget during the summer after my junior year when, after apprising my friends of my plans to begin campaigning in the fall, I was told that, "I was following the 'worst life plan' ever," and that, "I would regret this mistake for the rest of my life." An insult here and a naysayer there was tolerable. But this definitely rocked me. The totality of disbelief in my candidacy was so immense that I began to believe they were right; maybe I was wasting my time, and that my chances of victory were slim to none.

Even to this day, I feel that there is a group of people in my community who are still out to get me. At the monthly board of education meetings, almost every suggestion I make is met with grunts and muted derision coming from a group of PTA mothers. I'm constantly sent a barrage of unkind emails, which I

---

[32] "Maine could make history with gay Governor, youngest out ..." 2014. 24 Oct. 2015
<http://www.advocate.com/politics/election/2014/06/11/maine-could-make-history-gay-governor-youngest-out-legislator>

enjoy collecting in a folder titled "Josh Hate Mail" written with condescending attacks concerning my "naïveté," my "callous disregard for authority," my "reckless and/or irresponsible conduct," and how they "have no desire to hear from me or vote for me." My most recent favorite was a Facebook post with the header "You're a carpetbagger," which I assume relates to my commuting from upstate New York (while attending Cornell University) down to Long Island for monthly board meetings. In any case, kudos to these folks for originality. And this May, while campaigning for re-election, my opponents went as far as to put flyers in individual residents' mailboxes (illegal- I'll touch on this later), slandering me to such an egregious level that one resident told me it was, "The nastiest attack ad he had seen in a long time."

What helped me get through the difficult times of my campaign, and what sustains me to this day, is a piece of advice I received from current New York State Comptroller Tom DiNapoli back in January 2011 of my senior year of high school. He told me: **in order to survive in politics, you need to have a "stomach of steel."** I realized early on that the "thick skin" I thought I had was only satisfactory to fend off mean remarks such as a quip about my outfit, or unfriendly acts like not getting invited to a party as most high school students face. But, a "stomach of steel" is exactly what you need to persevere in the face of personal insults and unrelenting criticism in the way you think and are trying to serve the public. **It's the ability to, as my mother tells me every morning, "Stay in your own lane," to take a deep breath, gather your composure, and charge forward through the smoldering wall of criticism with the force of the Concorde.**

Moneyball is one of my favorite movies, and a quote from the movie which deeply resonates with me was something Boston Red Sox Owner John Henry said to Oakland Athletics General Manager Billy Beane regarding his unorthodox managerial style. Henry said:

"I know you've taken it in the teeth out there, but the first guy through the wall. It always gets bloody, always. It's the threat of not just the way of doing business, but in their minds it's threatening the game. But really what it's threatening is their livelihoods, it's threatening their jobs, it's threatening the way that they do things. And every time that happens, whether it's the government or a way of doing business or whatever it is, the people are holding the reins, have their hands on the switch. They go bat sh*t crazy."[33]

The more you deviate from the norm (running for office at a young age is one of the biggest deviations from the norm you can take), and the more you challenge the status quo, the tougher it will get. I have found that the only defense is to develop a "stomach of steel," continue to remind yourself that you are running for the right reasons, that you are trying to make a difference in your community and to serve the interests of the people you'll represent, remain true to who you are, run your race and do not pay any mind to those who solely want to tear you down. Do this and regardless of the outcome on Election Day, you will emerge a winner.

---

[33] "Moneyball (2011) - Quotes - IMDb." 2008. 24 Oct. 2015 <http://www.imdb.com/title/tt1210166/quotes>

However, in addition to intestinal fortitude, what helped me weather adversity during my campaign was my own personal support system—my family. Politics is a dirty business. You are human, and will most certainly take offense to things that are said about you and done to you. **Whether it's your family, your boyfriend or girlfriend, your best friends, or your teachers or your classmates, a personal support system is crucial to being able to run an effective race.**

Not all criticism is malicious however, and receiving feedback in the form of constructive criticism is definitely important. There is no substitute for life experience, and numerous times during my tenure on the board, I've received suggestions from adults that I've implemented into my routine as an elected official. In fact, one of those suggestions was to start a high school internship program for my re-election campaign, which resulted in dozens of high schoolers gaining experience in grassroots campaigning.

I follow the counsel of my younger brother Justin in having a "hand-in-the-sand" mentality when it comes to the advice of others. He analogizes and figures out which items of criticism to accept and reject like picking up sand in your hand at the beach. He says he uses this method, **"Where I take advice from everyone, and most of the advice I let slip through my fingers, but with the stuff that really resonates, I keep in the palm of my hand."**[34]

Your job as an elected official is to listen to all of your constituents. But, as people will undoubtedly give

[34] "Millennial Spotlight: Justin Lafazan - The Motivated Millennial." 2015. 24 Oct. 2015 <http://www.themotivatedmillennial.com/blog/millennial-spotlight-justin-lafazan>

you conflicting advice, absorb everything that residents have to say, and decide for yourself what to utilize and what to let go of.

I was relieved to learn that 100% of the young elected officials I interviewed for this book told me that they also felt running for office at a young age was difficult, and this difficulty was by no means solely attributed to fending off detractors and criticism.

As President Theodore Roosevelt proclaimed, **"Nothing in the world is worth having or worth doing unless it means effort, pain, difficulty... I have never in my life envied a human being who led an easy life. I have envied a great many people who led difficult lives and led them well."**[35]

Ellen Nesbitt says being an underdog made her race for Dutchess County Legislator difficult. Ellen was at a steep enrollment disadvantage. As the Republican candidate, she ran in a district with a Democratic to Republican enrollment ratio of 3:1. She says that, "When I told my dad I wanted to run, they had just re-districted, and he didn't want me to do it." She continues that when she, "Talked to different friends of ours, they told me 'you can't win this district—you don't have the numbers.'" Though her dad was skeptical, her mom was more optimistic. Ellen's mom told her dad that, "You need to just let her run...you [Ellen] want to do something and have a passion, you need to do this...there's always a chance you could lose." Though her mom was open to the possibility of losing, people in the legislature were feeling certain of it. Ellen recalls how, "Nobody in the legislature thought we were going

[35] "Nothing in the world is worth having or worth doing unless it ..." 2012. 24 Oct. 2015 <http://www.goodreads.com/quotes/312751-nothing-in-the-world-is-worth-having-or-worth-doing>

to win." They were wrong; Ellen won two primaries (the Conservative and the Independence parties), and went on to win the general election.

When asked whether it was difficult being a young candidate for a position held almost exclusively by adults, Chase Harrison from Millburn, New Jersey, responded "absolutely." Chase was frustrated by constant questioning regarding his "legitimacy" as a candidate, which pre-empted his ability to talk about his platform. Chase says that, "Before I could delve into the many issues I wanted to feature in my campaign, I had to answer the same questions about legitimacy repeatedly...voters wondered if it was legal for me to serve on certain committees, if I could be a student and a board member, if I understood how budgets worked, etc..."

This is an important point that Chase makes. When I ran in 2012, my critics constantly alleged that I was turning the election into a "circus" because as a teenager I wasn't a legitimate candidate for a position held by "mature adults." (Yes, this literally was one of the selling points my opposition used on their campaign literature.) So, on the one hand, you had an 18-year-old candidate who took major issue with the way the district functioned and articulated a vision to enhance the district for both students and taxpayers. On the other hand, you had a formidable group of "mature adults" disseminating rumors, lies, and *ad hominem* attacks about the teenaged candidate because they felt he didn't belong in the race. So, I once again pose the question I asked when I began campaigning in 2011; who's really causing the "circus?" **Do not let anyone challenge your "legitimacy" as a candidate because of your youth, or let them tell you that you don't "belong" in the race.** The beauty of our democracy is that we have a citizen-run government;

every single person who meets the age requirement is a "legitimate" candidate, and if you desire to step up and serve your community and those people who reside in it, then I promise that you most certainly "belong" in that race.

Chase also says that there was an unfair burden placed on him as opposed to the older candidates to prove he was knowledgeable on the issues. He says, "There was a notion that I had to prove expertise on every issue...none of the other candidates were expected to have the same level of knowledge about the budget, the staff, the curriculum, the budget, the buildings, the technology." **Chase handled this pressure put upon him by being *the most* prepared candidate, which is a crucial lesson to take from his campaign.** He feels that, "Because voters were looking for reasons to call my legitimacy and maturity into question, I had to be the most well-read and most adult of any of the candidates."

Doug Pascarella, of Plainedge, Long Island, when describing the difficulty of his campaign, called his candidacy an "uphill battle." Though president of his senior class at Plainedge High School when he ran for his school board, Doug says as a high school student you have "very little credibility" compared to adults with an established track record of community volunteerism. Doug took an interesting approach to easing residents' worries about his age. He consistently clarified to voters that he was running for just one seat on the board, and would by no means be making decisions on his own. Doug says he made it a point to re-assure voters that, "I would only be 1 of 7 members of the board of education, so I wouldn't have full control of board." He reminded voters, however, that he would certainly "share ideas and help board members come to consensus." This is a campaign tactic I adopted in my race (remember, I had Doug as a coach.) Through Facebook, I would private message Doug with questions each week, and stop by his office at least once a month to check in regarding my communication strategies. He reminded me to articulate to voters that a Syosset School Board made up of nine 18 year olds was not a wise idea, **but that *one* 18 year old, with fresh ideas, a unique perspective, and an ability to think outside of the box would certainly make an effective trustee.**

Moorestown New Jersey's Brandon Pugh felt the level of competition in his race made it difficult to be a young candidate. Brandon says that historically in his town, "School elections were generally non-competitive, with three or four candidates running for three seats." In Brandon's year; nine candidates for three seats. He believes his candidacy may have spurred adult candidates to run for the board, with the attitude that, "If a 19 year old can run, why can't I?" Brandon responded to this difficult level of competition by making the mission of his campaign to, "Speak with as many residents as possible." He believes that, "A lot of time people can't name any of the current serving board of education members, so as a candidate the most important thing you can do is tell people who you are and what you stand for." Moreover, he continues, **"If you're younger and may not have an established reputation in your community, it is essential you get out there and make up the difference."**

For West Virginia's Saira Blair, the rigors of the campaign trail made life as a high school senior difficult. Saira says that if she didn't have her father, West Virginia Senator Craig Blair, as her mentor, "The campaign would have been even more difficult." Saira recalls how, "Campaigning during my senior year of high school meant I had to miss out on normal high school activities." An example she gives is that she, "Had to give up time with my friends at the movies in order to write hand-written letters to potential voters." Looking back, Saira says the sacrifice was "definitely worth it." However, it is well worth noting that running for office means great personal sacrifice; **you're the CEO of your campaign, and it becomes one of your life's largest and most pressing priorities**. Saira says that she even, "Had to miss both my proms in order to participate in the 'youth in government' event." I remember not being able to go on vacation with my friends during spring break of my senior year in high school because I needed to knock on doors and collect signatures in order to get on the ballot. Yet looking back, I couldn't agree more with Saira when she says that the sacrifices are "definitely worth it."

    Yes, it was important to impress upon you the difficulty associated with running for office as a young candidate. But by no means am I suggesting that you hide from your youth. On the contrary, I urge you to leverage your youth, which is what makes you a unique candidate, and use it to your advantage. Many believe age is a barrier for entry into the political life. **There are a myriad of assumed barriers to entry in this world. Do not run away from these barriers—run into them and they will disappear!** Yes, I'm young. Yes, I don't have as much life experience as candidate Smith or candidate Jones. But I have fresh ideas. I have a unique perspective. I have an ability to think outside of the box. And nobody will work harder than me to serve my community. Yes, I'm young, and I'm not going to apologize for it. This is me; this is who I am, this is what I stand for, this is what I'm going to do once elected, and this is why you should cast your vote for me.

Connor Kurtz, hailing from Amity Township, Pennsylvania, adopted this mantra to perfection. Connor says that because he had more time than those with full-time jobs and families, he, "Campaigned more than the adults did." He says that, "Being young, my voice was amplified, and I had a lot of attention given to me because of my age." Connor, though utilizing his age to attract attention to his campaign, didn't make age the centerpiece of his story. He advises to, "Make voters and the media understand that your campaign is not about age but about ideas... **age doesn't define me, my ideas and my morals define me.**" Connor believes voters appreciated his "zeal and passion to improve the school district." His message to residents was that, "This school district made me the person I am today, and I would love the opportunity to give back." Voters responded well to Connor's approach; the *Reading Eagle,* a local Berks County, Pennsylvania newspaper, ran an editorial after he won on May 26th, 2011, which read that, "People liked not only the message but the messenger."[36]

---

[36] "High School Student's Primary Win Brings Many Lessons." 2015. 20 Oct. 2015 <http://www2.readingeagle.com/article.aspx?id=310412>

Tips

#1 Do NOT put literature in individual residents' mailboxes-that is illegal. The U.S. Postal Inspection Service clearly states that, "Mailboxes are considered federal property."[37] If you knock on a resident's door and they are home, hand them a piece of your literature as you introduce yourself (we'll get into more detail in a bit). If a resident is not home, simply hang the piece of literature on their doorknob. A trick I've learned is to punch a hole in the top of the piece of paper, tie a rubber band through it, and use the rubber band as a door hanger (have to learn how to stretch a buck!).

#2 Watch videos of how seasoned politicians display their "stomach of steel" when faced with hecklers and criticizers during public forums. Whether you choose to take the diplomatic route of President Barack Obama, the combative style of Governor Chris Christie, the idiosyncratic style of Donald Trump, or your own style that you develop, be prepared to face negativity and let it go in one ear and out the other.

#3 Like Doug Pascarella suggests, you may find it advantageous to remind voters that you're running for just one seat on your board of education/town council/county legislature, as opposed to running to be an executive. Remind voters that you have fresh ideas, you can think outside of the box, and that your unique perspective will allow you to be an effective elected official.

---

[37] "Protecting Yourself from Mailbox Vandalism." 2011. 24 Oct. 2015 <https://postalinspectors.uspis.gov/raddocs/tipvandl.htm>

#4 An approach I recommend to handling advice from others is my brother Justin's "hand-in-the-sand" mentality. He says that he uses this method, "Where I take advice from everyone, and most of the advice I let slip through my fingers, but with the stuff that really resonates, I keep in the palm of my hand."

#5 Don't let an enrollment disadvantage dissuade you from running for office. Ellen Nesbitt was at a 3:1 enrollment disadvantage and won her general election.

#6 Having a high school internship program will be a great benefit to your campaign. High school students are some of the brightest and most dedicated individuals I've ever campaigned with. Often times they are looking for avenues to both gain experience and enhance their resumes, so your campaign will be a great fit for them. Talk to the high school debate team, talk to the Young Democrats and Republicans, talk to everybody; the more people who touch your campaign the better your odds of winning on Election Day.

Chapter Summary

- **Young candidates are almost always surrounded by an immense cloud of doubt over whether they can actually win a race.** Running for office at a young age is an incredibly difficult undertaking; 100% of the elected officials interviewed for this book agreed.

- **I found Comptroller Tom DiNapoli's advice to develop a "stomach of steel" to be one of the most crucial pieces of advice I've used in both of my campaigns.** We are all human, and thus inevitably all sensitive to some degree, meaning that some of the attacks will hurt. It's those individuals who are able to continue to charge forward with integrity in their actions, with concrete ideas, and with sharp focus in spite of these attacks who prevail in elections.

- **You can never have too strong of a handle on the issues**. Do your homework on anything that might come up in a conversation with a resident, or in a public forum. As Chase Harrison from Millburn, New Jersey says, "Because voters were looking for reasons to call my legitimacy and maturity into question, I had to be the most well- read and most adult of any of the candidates."

- **The more you deviate from the norm (running for office at a young age is one of the biggest deviations from the norm you can take), and the more you challenge the status quo, the tougher it will get.** I have found that the only defense is to develop a "stomach of steel." Continue to remind yourself that you are running for the right reasons, you are trying to make a difference in your community and to serve the interests of the people you'll represent, remain true to who you are, run your race and do not pay any mind to those who solely want to tear you down. Do this, and regardless of the vote tally, you emerge a winner.

- **When things get difficult, remember President Theodore Roosevelt's words**; "nothing in the world is worth having or worth doing unless it means effort, pain, difficulty... I have never in my life envied a human being who led an easy life. I have envied a great many people who led difficult lives and led them well."

Walk Before You Run

You've made the choice to run. And you understand the impending difficulty of running for office at a young age. This chapter is about getting involved in your community *before* you begin campaigning.

When you run for office, you are seeking an opportunity to serve your community. Therefore something I, and countless young elected officials I speak to across the country recommend, is to get involved in your community before you run for office. This can be in the form of community service, volunteering on a campaign, political party activism, advocating for a cause, involvement in a school club or group, serving in student government, or a myriad of other ways. **I stand firm in saying that it's your willingness to get involved now at a local level, throwing your energy into any worthwhile cause, that are the building blocks of your life success.**

Now, of course you are not disqualified from running for office because you have no history of community service. For example, Ellen Nesbitt says, "I wasn't involved in my community too much before running...the most exposure I had was through sports at my high school and getting to know people through there. My brothers (11 and 13 at the time) were very active in little league and have been since they were 5, so I knew other people from going to their games as well." Remember that Ellen, without this history of community involvement, still went on to overcome a 3:1 enrollment disadvantage and win her general election.

However, significant involvement in your community will unequivocally enhance your credibility.

    This chapter will share how I, and several of the young elected officials in this book, got involved in our communities before we ran for office. Linus Pauling, a historic scientist and humanitarian, once proclaimed that, **"The best way to have a good idea is to have a lot of ideas."** If one or many examples mentioned here pique your interest, run with it! A good idea in one community is more likely than not a good idea in another community, and good ideas are meant to be replicated.

    Seattle's Cyrus Habib is among those who implore Millennials to join community organizations. He says community organizations are, "Dying to have young people involved...get on the board of any non-profit that matches your values: parks' board, planning commission...**build that civic resume**."

    This concept of a "civic resume" is vital to establishing your credibility as a young person seeking elected office. It is incredibly difficult to compete with the professional resumes of adults; even if you have interned or worked in the past, they most likely have a head start by a few decades. However, you most definitely can compete with older adults when it comes to a "civic resume," because although they've spent more time in the professional world, as a young person you have more time available to dedicate to your community. Cyrus feels that, "Voters want to see it [civic resume], you'll learn more, and you'll develop your list of community endorsers that are especially important when you're young." He uses the example of a school superintendent as a possible community endorser. (But, clearly I didn't have the blessings of my former superintendent on Election Day!) Cyrus explains that, "To have the superintendent of schools to support you as an early candidate for the board of education is a really great endorsement...you get that endorsement because you volunteered on a committee, etc...., putting yourself in a great spot."

Once again, I will make this clear; if you have no history of community service yet you still want to run, my hat goes off to you, and I am always here to help you. However, I share the sentiments Cyrus articulates when it comes to getting involved in your community before running for office.

Cyrus says that, **"I think that people view running for office as the first step...it's really the third step...be strategic, and spend a couple of years positioning yourself."** He continues, "Don't run this year, run in two years, and spend these two years getting yourself out there...don't run now, set the stage." Cyrus says that this is not only advantageous when it comes to building a "civic resume," but it is also a benefit "from a media perspective." He explains that, "When the media refers to you, they are going to use a description, or a term to describe you...be clear about what that is going to be...are you tech entrepreneur Cyrus Habib, Democratic Party activist Cyrus Habib, civil rights lawyer Cyrus Habib?" He advises to, "Work backwards from that, dress for the job you want to have, and when the media does describe you, you own that title...maybe community leader Cyrus Habib because you're involved in your community, and now people see that as your title and give you more credibility."

Like Cyrus, Carteret School Board's Daniel Croson got involved in his community at a young age, and maintains that the key to getting your foot in the door is always volunteering:

"Town-sponsored events such as carnivals, health clinics, or concerts, as well as political causes like rallies, canvassing, or poll working are all great places to plug in; anything at all to begin demonstrating your commitment to the community. Identify your municipality, county, or district's event coordinator, and make yourself their most dependable volunteer. **They say that 80% of success is just showing up; so start showing up and watch what happens.**"

Daniel says he was involved with a number of community organizations and events which he says, "Served to prepare me and broaden my perspective for elected office." He continues that, "From Planning Board Vice Chairman to Secretary of the local political organization and everything in between, my resume was strengthened and my relationships with key stakeholders were forged to the point in which I was recruited as a candidate."

This is a key point that Daniel brings up. When elections are partisan, and party labels appear on the ballot, the decision makers in that political party often endorse candidates they want to see as their party's representative in the general election. This endorsement, as Daniel received when he was recruited as a candidate, can be advantageous for several reasons. First, it can dissuade another member of your party from running for that position, thus avoiding a primary election. Secondly, it can instill confidence in voters that you have the party's full support. Lastly, it can give you access to resources such as volunteers and campaign contributions that you may not have as an outsider. Now, to make myself very, very clear here; I am not, by any means, promoting getting this endorsement if it means sacrificing your principles, relinquishing your independence, and becoming a "party hack." **It's our generation who I firmly believe will make these types of politicians an extinct species, and put them in the Smithsonian where they belong.** But if you and the party leaders agree on the core values you hold, and they support you being an independent representative of the residents you will serve, then this endorsement as a young candidate makes a lot of sense.

This is congruent with the course of action Montana's Daniel Zolnikov took when he was a political neophyte. As mentioned in Chapter 1, Daniel sought out those who were politically involved at the beginning of his exploration of a candidacy. He found out that "we [the local party leaders] were pretty like-minded in some areas" and as the Republican Party was looking for candidates, they, "Asked me to run for a seat."

A point to keep in mind throughout this book; while the experiences of young vs. adult candidates differ dramatically, there is great overlap between the experiences of the young elected officials in this book.

Whether you're 25 and have spent the past three years after graduation managing a community non-profit to feed the homeless, or you're a 21-year-old college student who heads up the Young Republicans, or you're an 18-year-old high schooler who serves in the student government, you have a proven record being involved and helping others in your community.

California's Das Williams is a young elected official who created quite the resume at a young age; he had a proven record of community involvement before graduating high school! Das' introduction to community participation came in the form of political campaigns. He says he, "Was 17 when I worked on my first political campaign for 3rd District Supervisor Bill Wallace and went on to work on almost 30 local elections." In addition to campaigns, he also worked for a local elected official. Das says he, "Worked for now-Senator, then-Assemblymember Hannah-Beth Jackson for 4 years while she represented this District." As he matured, Das' service transitioned from working for others in politics to working for causes in politics. Though now as Assemblyman, "Prior to being elected to the Assembly, I served for six years on the Santa Barbara City Council." It was on the City Council that he, "Worked as a community organizer for the local advocacy non-profit, CAUSE." He also, "Served as a trustee for Peabody Charter School in Santa Barbara, among many other boards of community organizations on which I served."

While Das was in his twenties when he ran for the Santa Barbara City Council, Connor Kurtz was in his teens when he decided to seek a seat on the Daniel Boone Area Board of School Directors in Pennsylvania. Connor says that before he ran for office his, "Community involvement was limited to attending school board meetings and doing occasional work as a volunteer hospice counselor." Most of Connor's involvement, "Came through the school system: student government, quiz bowl, and the small debate club I founded." In addition to being an active member of the student body in terms of extra-curricular activities, he was without a doubt active when it came to advocacy. Connor, "Was a very outspoken opponent of commercial television advertising in school. I saw it as a waste of money and—more importantly—valuable instructional time." This would become one of the focal points of his platform during his eventual candidacy. A few weeks after his campaign began, he says that, "A long-dormant taxpayer community advocacy group experienced a resurgence and I became their first 'student member.'" He recalls that, "The chairman [a gentleman named Rich Martino] sent me an email, I laid out my campaign's platform, and he supported me...we struck up a friendship and began strategizing how to expand the new pro-taxpayer, pro-student school board majority." Mr. Martino went from a supporter of Connor's to a colleague; Connor tells me that, "Two years later, I convinced him to run for the board. We put together a team and swept the election."

How did the story of Rich's and Connor's relationship end? Connor was elected as the temporary president for the board's 2013 reorganizational meeting at which time he swore-in the new board members. He then, "Cast the deciding vote to make Rich the board president, and I was elected vice president."

New Jersey's Anthony Fasano is a hybrid between Das and Connor.

Like Das, Anthony expanded his community involvement outside the walls of his high school and into the broader community. He says that, "Before I ran for office I co-founded a youth-mediated charitable organization for troubled children ages 12-21 in my hometown of Hopatcong called: NJ Outreach." Anthony tells me that NJ Outreach started, "When my old soccer coach came to me and asked for help with starting a small charitable organization through our local church." Anthony handled the social media, weekend activities, and making speeches on behalf of the organization. He recalls this as, "Probably my first experience in true civic involvement and it eventually led to my decision to run for the board of education."

But like Connor, Anthony was very involved as a student in school. He was a part of, "18 clubs and organizations in high school" including football, tennis, and National Honor Society. During that time, he also coached football and tutored young students in math and history. He says however that, "The biggest reason I ran for the board was because of my experience as class president in high school." Anthony continues that, "It was that experience that made me realize we, as a community, could be doing a much better job at ensuring the district can advance and promote student achievement for the modern student in Hopatcong."

Adversity early on in Brandon Pugh's life was the precursor for getting involved in his community as a young adult. Brandon, also a New Jersey native, says, "Growing up I had a somewhat unique childhood, as I was unable to speak until I was after five years old, along with having severe learning disabilities." He continues that, "My parents and I were told that there were slim chances that my condition would improve...however, **very few people know about my past because I overcame these difficulties, but they created a deeply instilled desire to help others since so many people assisted me.**" Overcoming these struggles allows Brandon to truly enjoy volunteering in his community and beyond. Like Connor, Brandon was a very active student in terms of volunteerism. He, "Took on various leadership positions while in high school, including school organizations/student government, school board committees, and community-based organizations." He remembers that two of his, "Favorite roles included serving as a volunteer and paid EMT, and previously serving as the president of the Interact Club."

Additionally, Brandon believes he, "Was fortunate to have had the opportunity to make various trips ranging from a couple weeks to several months for humanitarian work, including to Argentina, the Czech Republic, Mexico, and Puerto Rico, among others locations." A trip of note was to Argentina, where for several months Brandon taught a first grade class and assisted with curriculum development. He believes,

"This is where I was first exposed to education outside of being a student myself, and I quickly realized that I had a passion for it." He turned this passion into action, and today is a passionate advocate for educational opportunities of all students in Moorestown.

Personally, I had been involved in my community since middle school. Whether it was operating the scoreboard for the Syosset Basketball League or refereeing for the Syosset Soccer Club, I always enjoyed being active in Syosset and meeting new people. My true community service however began my senior year of high school, when I founded Safe Ride Syosset, Inc.

Drunk driving was, and continues to be, an epidemic everywhere, especially on Long Island. Unlike the majority of my classmates in high school, I didn't have my first drink of alcohol until I turned 21. So when I got my driver's license during my junior year in high school, I immediately became the default designated driver on the weekends. Worrying about getting my classmates home safe, I would frequently drive 10-15 kids home a night. But for a graduating class of over 600 kids, what about the rest of my classmates? How were they getting home? Who was looking out for them? I knew I wanted to act, but I struggled with how.

My epiphany came when then-Jets Wide Receiver Braylon Edwards was arrested for DWI in September of 2010. Edwards, like every player on the Jets roster, was eligible for the "Player Protect program," which "provides a 24-hour driving service exclusively for professional athletes."[39] So if Edwards, with millions of dollars, the support of the entire Jets

---

[39] "New York Jets' Braylon Edwards charged with drunken driving." 2015. 24 Oct. 2015 <http://sports.espn.go.com/nfl/news/story?id=5598872>

organization, and the accessibility of the "Player Protect program" could still make the stupid decision to drink and drive, what about my Syosset High School classmates? What were their options if they got stuck in an emergency situation and needed a safe ride home? Thus, Safe Ride Syosset was born.

The crux of Safe Ride was that Syosset High School students who either drank, or were driven by someone who drank, could call the Safe Ride hotline on Friday and Saturday nights from 10:00 p.m. until 2:00 a.m. Then either I or Safe Ride's volunteer drivers were dispatched to go pick these kids up and take them home free of charge, no questions asked, and no judgements passed. Safe Ride's drivers were Syosset High School seniors, working with a sober "buddy" for the evening. Our entire program was volunteer, and run by students for students. Our drivers volunteered their time, and paid for their own gas. We found that kids feared getting caught drinking by their parents more than hurting themselves or others on the road. For this reason, Safe Ride was a confidential service, and no adults were involved.

In 2012 alone we drove home 350 students safely. Equally as important, we helped take kids who were part of the problem and turn them into part of the solution. Safe Ride drivers would volunteer one night every other month to abstain from drugs and alcohol and drive their peers home. We were able to successfully teach an entire class of students that there is a discernable and imperative difference between drinking, and drinking and driving.

Starting Safe Ride was quite the learning lesson. At first, I was Safe Ride Syosset's lone volunteer driver. I found that high school seniors weren't very excited about giving up a night of their weekend to both be sober and drive their classmates home. This was frustrating, as I alone drove every Friday and Saturday night for about a month. Yet it was during this early stage that I found the core of Safe Ride's drivers; I was able to persuade those who had used Safe Ride for a ride home to give back and drive for it. Was it weird having a student on Friday night in the back of my car being driven home, and then having that same student drive others home on Saturday? At first, very weird. However this became the norm, and a great learning opportunity for students about giving back to their community.

A major problem I encountered was that I wasn't allowed to advertise the program's availability during the school day or at school events. This ties back into having a stomach of steel. I was told by the high school that I wasn't allowed to advertise Safe Ride because it was an "outside group," and that the district didn't let any outside groups advertise in its buildings. This, not to my surprise in the slightest, was blatantly false; I'd walk the halls each day and see a poster for an outside group, or a club would bring an outside group to its meetings to address students. The truth of the matter was that Syosset's superintendent felt that the more public exposure Safe Ride received, the more of an advantage I would have in my election. Never mind the safety of the students, right? If you're skeptical, let me tell you about a specific incident.

Former Nassau County District Attorney Kathleen Rice held a program at Syosset High School called *Choices and Consequences,* which was given to parents of new drivers as well as students. The main goal of this program was to ensure that no teen got behind the wheel of a car while drunk, or got in the car with a drunk driver. Being that this program held the same goal of Safe Ride Syosset, I contacted DA Rice's office to speak at the event.

I was told, because Syosset was hosting the event, that I would be allowed to speak during the presentation if the district agreed as well. But when I asked the district if I could speak, in order to let several hundred high school students and parents know of this brand new service offered to the community, I was denied.

Seldom in my life do I accept "no" as an answer. In fact, from a young age my father has taught me that, "No only means no when it comes to women." I have and always will always fight to find a solution to a problem. So while I wasn't allowed to present to the parents in attendance, I decided to do the next best thing—I put flyers on the windshields of every attendee's car detailing what Safe Ride was, why they should talk to their children about its availability, and listed the hotline number. Now, did the principal threaten to suspend me after he found out? Yes. For a kid who to this day has never had a minute of detention in his life (I remind my mother of this statistic when she's mad at me), this was frightening. But the moral of this story is twofold; first, when you are a candidate for office or you are an elected official, there is heightened scrutiny placed on you, and you get treated differently than when you were just a citizen. **Secondly, and equally as important, is that when you run for office you have to, as my grandmother says, have a little "chutzpah," or have courage.** Calculated risks can pay great dividends, as putting flyers on these cars did for me; Safe Ride doubled the amount of calls it received the following week.

Lastly, I faced a ton of criticism from adults in my community about Safe Ride. The main charge against my program was that Safe Ride promoted teen drinking because it was, as the critics labeled it, a "free taxi service" for kids who drank to take advantage of.

I will link back to this later, but when you present an idea and are passionate about it, the only way to beat back detractors is to remain steadfastly behind your idea. I would be active on blogs, on social media, and even in the local diner defending my program. Ad nauseam I would recite the talking points I crafted about how kids were going to drink with or without Safe Ride's existence. But wouldn't we rather our students have a safe alternative to a drunk driver in case of an emergency?

My detractors still exist to this day, criticizing me on a range of issues. If you in your heart know that what you are doing is right, then forget them and move on. One of my favorite quotes sums up the way I feel on this issue; as Abraham Lincoln said, **"Be sure you put your feet in the right place, then stand firm."**

Safe Ride Syosset was the genesis for involvement in my community. Yet how I began my career in politics is quite different.

Unlike many, politics did not run in the Lafazan family. My dad is a mortgage banker and my mom is a psychotherapist. Since kindergarten, every May for the school board and budget vote, and every November for the general election, my parents would take me into the voting booth with them. Thus, I was always aware of the prevalence of local politics and the importance of democratic participation. But my dad, unlike Ian Calderon's or Ellen Nesbitt's or Saira Blair's, wasn't a politician. Unlike Cyrus Habib, my mom never ran for judge.

So how did I get involved in politics? In the words of the contemporary philosopher

Aubrey Graham, colloquially hailed as Drake, I most definitely, "Started from the bottom."[40]
It takes serious cash to attend a political fundraiser or a civic organization's gala, and unfortunately it's pretty rare for there to be a student discount! Therefore I reached out to countless political groups from both sides of the aisle who were hosting events, and asked if I could volunteer my time at their event in exchange for attending. I went to dozens of events and checked coats, sold raffles, registered guests, ran logistics, and even at one point experienced my first stint as a waiter. Any job that is essential for an event to run smoothly I did. And after I was done with my assigned job, I was now a regular guest at the event; the only difference was that I was almost always the youngest person in the room by several decades.
Though tough at first, I developed the courage to go up to the "bigwigs" at these functions and introduce myself. **This goes hand-in-hand with one of the themes of this book-leverage your youth! You are young, and therefore have an excuse to talk to any guest in attendance at any function you go to.** For example:

Hi, Mr. County Executive, my name is Josh Lafazan. I'm a junior at Syosset High School, and I'm considering running for the Syosset School Board of Education next year. I would love to hear about the beginning of your career in politics, and what advice you have for first-time candidates.

Or you can try:

---

[40] "DRAKE LYRICS - Started From The Bottom - A-Z Lyrics." 2013. 24 Oct. 2015
<http://www.azlyrics.com/lyrics/drake/startedfromthebottom.html>

Good evening, Ms. (insert last name of the Executive Director of the organization), my name is Josh Lafazan. I think your organization does great work, and I'm looking to get more involved in the community. How would you recommend I go about contributing to your organization?

After a myriad of these conversations, I would wake up the next morning and send them a follow-up email. Oh yes, make sure to ask them for their business card or contact info!

Dear Mr. Obama, it was great to meet you last night at the White House. I really appreciated your advice on campaigning, and enjoyed your stories about your days playing ball at Harvard. If it's alright with you, I'd like to reach out to you in the future for guidance and mentorship. With appreciation, Josh Lafazan. P.S. Hope Malia and Sasha are enjoying summer camp!

From establishing these connections, I am now blessed with individuals whom I reach out to freely for counsel. Most adults (I say *most* because some will want to tear you down solely because you're young and ambitious. It's important to spot these people early on), are receptive to helping youths they see as motivated. **An important recommendation that I received early on and will now share with you is: to ask for *advice*, and not for a favor.** It is displeasing when you ask someone for something, let alone when you don't really know them. But it's perfectly acceptable to ask for advice. Moreover, once you make a connection with someone they will be more inclined to help you.

Mentors have played such an instrumental role in my life; I wouldn't have had my successes without them. And there are no better mentors than those who have already achieved what you are looking to achieve. To again quote my little brother Justin (yes, mom, I'm trying to earn brownie points here), "We need to ask ourselves this question: what do we need to get from where we are to where we want to be, both personally, and professionally? Surround yourself with the people who are doing what you want to be doing, and learn how they achieved what you want to achieve."[41]

I am writing this book because for the past few years I have been able to mentor some amazing Millennials who have turned out to make fantastic young elected officials, from this book's Anthony Fasano, to Peter Mountanos, who, at 18, was elected to the Wantagh School Board on Long Island in 2013.[42] I wanted to share the knowledge and experience that I gained going through my "school of hard knocks" during the campaign and my first term on the board. This book was the way for me to do so.

So that's my start, both in my community and the political world. Looking back, I can't believe that my journey hadn't even yet begun.

---

[41] "Mantra — Justin Lafazan." 2015. 24 Oct. 2015
<http://www.justinlafazan.com/mantra/>
[42] "Peter Mountanos, 18, joins Wantagh school board | Newsday." 2013.
24 Oct. 2015 <http://www.newsday.com/long-island/nassau/peter-mountanos-18-joins-wantagh-school-board-1.5615867>

Tips

#1 An important recommendation that I received early on is to ask for advice and not for a favor. It is displeasing when you ask someone for something, let alone when you don't really know them. However it's perfectly acceptable to ask for advice. Moreover, once you make that connection, they will be more inclined to help you.

#2 Do you see a problem in your community? Starting a nonprofit is an excellent way to define the problem, and strategically attack it. NJ Outreach and Safe Ride Syosset are examples of nonprofits that made a genuine impact in Hopatcong, NJ and Syosset, NY respectively.

#3 A great way to meet the political heavyweights is at events. If the mayor is speaking at a party event, or the executive director of an organization is being honored at a gala, you can definitely get face time with them, even if for just a short while. If you're like me and don't have the means to attend by writing a check, reach out in advance and offer to volunteer your time in exchange for attending. Few organizations will turn you down.

#4 Daniel Croson got involved in his community at a young age, and maintains that the key to getting your foot in the door is always volunteering. He reminds young candidates that, "They say that 80% of success is just showing up; so start showing up and watch what happens."

#5 Get a business card or an email address from anybody that you meet. Following up with them after you first meet is in my opinion just as important as your first impression.

Chapter Summary

- **"Starting from the bottom" was an experience I cherish and will never forget.** Having gone from somebody who checked coats at an event to being an invited guest at the head table was the highlight of this journey. And that is exactly what this will be for you: a journey. Entering politics as a neophyte will make you hungrier to achieve success, and much more appreciative of it when you achieve it. When you do something all on your own, nobody can discredit you or take it away from you.

- **Cyrus Habib is among those who implore you to join community organizations.** He says community organizations are, "Dying to have young people involved...get on the board of any non-profit that matches your values...parks' board, planning commission...build that civic resume."

- **Leverage your youth!** You are young, and therefore have an excuse to talk to any guest in attendance at any function you go to. These connections will be invaluable to you in terms of building a trusted group of advisors whom you can rely on for sound counsel and guidance.

- **A point to keep in mind throughout this book;** while the experiences of young vs. adult candidates differ dramatically, there is great overlap between the experiences of the young elected officials in this book.

- **You do NOT need to have a family connection in politics to successfully run for office.** Does it make your first campaign easier? You bet. But is it a prerequisite? Absolutely not. President Obama was born to a single mom.[43] Speaker Boehner is the son of a bartender.[44]

[43] "Family | The White House." 2009. 24 Oct. 2015
<https://www.whitehouse.gov/issues/family>
[44] "John Boehner: From Bartender's Son to Would be House ..." 2013. 24
Oct. 2015 <http://www.foxnews.com/politics/2010/11/03/john-
boehner-from-bartender-son-to-would-be-house-speaker/>

It's All About the Issues

I was a stellar athlete...if you take into account my basketball statistics through the sixth grade (my inherited athletic ability disallowed a professional career—I forgive you, mom and dad). I am an avid sports fan, and have loved playing sports ever since I was young. Sports teach life lessons the way few activities can; the ideals of hard work, leadership, trust in others. For me, I loved sports because I'm incredibly competitive.

But politics is the most competitive activity I've ever participated in. And unlike some sports, everybody can compete in politics regardless of inherited ability, whether you're a past WWE wrestler like former Minnesota Governor Jesse Ventura, or you're in a wheelchair like Texas Governor Greg Abbott. **Because politics is a competition of ideas.**[45]

It's a competition of principles and ideals; a competition of the visions that people have for a community, for a state, or even a country. And the best part about this competition? The judges that decide who wins are your neighbors.

This chapter is about those ideas you will raise during your campaign.

When you run for office, you are presenting a plan of action you would take when elected—this is

---

[45] "Why the competition of ideas matters." 2014. 10 Nov. 2015 <https://www.aei.org/publication/why-the-competition-of-ideas-matters/>

referred to as your "platform." Running for office because you simply want to hold that title of board trustee or town councilman is not enough; **holding an office is a privilege, and you need to do something in it to make a difference.**

For me, the biggest issue on my mind was the lack of transparency and open government in our school district.

We had a budget just shy of $200 Million dollars, yet the only Syosset residents who were able to view the budget were sitting members of the school board of education.

To me this was nonsensical.

Taxpayers were anteing up some of the highest property taxes in the United States for the school district; shouldn't they be able to see where the money was going?[46]

Next, residents who had questions on school district matters were allowed to address the superintendent and the school board during the "audience to the public" segment of the monthly school board meetings. The only problem was that these questions could only be related to items on that evening's agenda, and thus all questions were based on items pre-authorized by the board!

As you probably would, I found this to be insane.

Third, in many districts when residents want basic documents and information, such as the enrollment total of the incoming kindergarten class or a certain district policy, they request it a board meeting. But since residents couldn't do that at a Syosset board meeting, they had to submit a FOIL request (Freedom

---

[46] "Highest property taxes in America - CNN Money." 2013. 10 Nov. 2015 <http://money.cnn.com/2013/11/25/pf/taxes/property-taxes/>

of Information Law Request) with the district.[47] A FOIL request "allows members of the public to access records of governmental agencies."[48] Can you imagine? Residents whose taxes paid the salary of the superintendent being told by her that they couldn't have certain information for no other reason other than secrecy. I even had to submit a FOIL request during my campaign for basic information I should have been able to get at a board meeting.

Lastly, Syosset is blessed with a wealth of professionals in all areas of industry and commerce. But these experts, along with the rest of the community, were shut out from assisting the district because unlike in other districts, where open community committees are available to the public, they weren't in Syosset.

None of this made sense to me.

And I'm thrilled to report that each of these four examples of lack of transparency in Syosset have since been reversed. Any citizen can now view the budget online, residents can ask any question they have at a board meeting, basic information and documents can be received at a monthly board meeting, and community residents are able to share their input with the district.

You see, there are a myriad of issues that you can raise, as each community sets different priorities. **Yet whatever issues appear on your platform, you must believe in them; remember that voters, like sharks and blood, can smell ingenuity from a mile away.**

---

[47] "Committee on Open Government - New York State ..." 2012. 10 Nov. 2015 <https://www.dos.ny.gov/coog/freedomfaq.html>

[48] "FOIL - New York State Education Department." 2014. 19 Nov. 2015 <http://www.nysed.gov/foil>

But with all these problems I recognized in Syosset, none of these issues were number one in the minds of my constituents. Rather, it was the fact that our superintendent, Dr. Carole Hankin, was the highest paid school administrator in New York State, collecting $506,000 in total compensation, and that our deputy superintendent, Dr. Jeffrey Streitman, made $382,382 in total compensation, far more than many *superintendents* across the state.[49]

This is a major lesson I learned early on about politics; your constituents set your priorities.

Of course you can have your own ideas on how to improve your community; these ideas may even be contrary to popular belief at the time. But you work for your constituents, and they set the top of your agenda. And the way you figure out what their priorities are is by talking to them *before* you run.

I spoke to over 100 residents when I was still in the exploratory phase of my campaign during my junior year in high school. Seldom did I meet a resident who failed to mention the salaries of either Dr. Hankin, Dr. Streitman, or both. Therefore, reigning in egregious administrative salaries became my number one priority. And it's remained so ever since.

In fact, in May of 2014, I cast the lone "no" vote to renew the contract of our deputy superintendent, Dr. Streitman.[50] I mention this because even after you're elected, your priorities still must remain in alignment with your constituents.

---

[49] "She's in a cla$$ by herself | New York Post." 2013. 2 Nov. 2015 <http://nypost.com/2011/03/06/shes-in-a-cla-by-herself/>
[50] "BOE Minutes/Agendas/Policies - Syosset Central School ..." 2014. 2 Nov. 2015
<http://www.syossetschools.org/boardofeducation/default.aspx>

But my platform also contained ideas which were completely unique from the ideas suggested by residents in the past.

I posed these ideas and sentiments on a flyer with the title "Syosset: Fight Back." **To this day, I'm a fighter; I'm hyper-passionate, and don't know any other way to operate. The beauty of politics is that voters like all different types of personalities in candidates; it's clear that you can be brash like Donald Trump, calm like Ben Carson, or grumpy like Bernie Sanders, and have success in the political arena.**[51]

I called for the implementation of computer coding instruction into Syosset's classrooms. I believe that learning to write basic computer code will become as fundamental as algebra is today. I argued that the speed with which our technology is growing will make every person without these skills seem illiterate in the world of computers 15 years from now. Computer programming jobs are growing at 2 times the national average, yet only a small portion of our students are currently leaving Syosset High School with these skills.[52] And with the burgeoning opportunities for computer programmers, only one in 10 U.S. schools currently teach children to code.[53] I wanted Syosset to

---

[51] "7 ways Bernie Sanders reminds us of our grumpy grandpa ..." 2015. 6 Nov. 2015 <https://www.washingtonpost.com/news/the-fix/wp/2015/07/22/7-times-bernie-sanders-reminds-us-of-our-grumpy-grandpa/>

[52] "Code.org Overview (PDF)." 2014. 10 Nov. 2015 <https://code.org/files/Code.orgOverview.pdf>

[53] "Teach Kids How To Code And You Give Them A Skill For Life." 2013. 10 Nov. 2015 <http://www.forbes.com/sites/nickmorrison/2013/12/27/teach-kids-how-to-code-and-you-give-them-a-skill-for-life/>

be forward-thinking, and give our students the very best chance at success in the tumultuous 21st century job market.

I called for a line item review of the district's budget, to be conducted by members of the community in their individual areas of expertise. I refer to these people as "captains of industry," as Syosset is home to some of the country's premiere business professionals. So, I wanted energy experts to look at our expenditures on oil and natural gas. I wanted our insurance experts to look at our insurance policies, finance experts to look at our outstanding bonds, and so on. Who's more motivated to save the district money than the taxpayers themselves? I argued that if these individuals found that the district had sound spending procedures in place, and was getting the best bang for its buck, then taxpayers would simply be given peace of mind, and all it would cost was the energy of our volunteers. And if these experts were able to save money, then it would be a win for both the district and taxpayers.

I called on the district to begin using directed donations to help fund capital projects. In Syosset, there were numerous organizations that had tried to donate funds for specific improvements within our school district. Yet the school district continued to deny the donors the opportunity, citing school policy against directed contributions. That made me beg the question—were we so rich as a school district to have this policy? **I argued that all the tax-paying citizens in our school district were fed up with the district's attitude that the money spigot would always be turned on.** Additionally, I contended that we should be looking to encourage donations from alumni, with these donations usually directed to their positive experiences at their schools. Many football players have gone back and donated a new turf field and improved locker rooms at their high schools. However if we had such a player in our district's history who wished to do this, he would be told "give us the money and we will decide what to do with it." In short, I believed that the arrogance that goes along with that type of policy must come to an end, and thus advocated that the district pass a resolution allowing projects to be funded by donations.[54]

Lastly, I called for our district to utilize green energy on a much larger scale. In Syosset, taxpayers shell out $3,000,000 annually for electric and natural gas alone. That's why I supported green energy initiatives with short 1-3 year ROI (return on investment periods). I argued that LED lighting was the first place to start. In addition, I felt that smart sensors, solar panels, and window treatments should all be explored. I believed, as I still do, that we should strive to be the greenest district on Long Island, both to save money and to teach our children the importance of caring for the environment.

There were many other issues that I supported in 2012, and I brought new issues into my re-election campaign in 2015. I've achieved success with some of my ideas, and I've struggled to implement others (will be discussed later). **But the ideas you champion, the concepts you support, and the vision you espouse, will define you as a candidate.**

What separates our generation, the Millennial generation, from the previous generations who serve in government is that we want to *do something*. We have a sense of urgency to get things *done*. We believe politics

---

[54] "Capital Construction Projects Funded by Donations or ... - p-12." 2010. 6 Nov. 2015
<http://www.p12.nysed.gov/facplan/articles/C07_projects_funded_by_donations.html>

is a vehicle for doing *good*, rather than partisan attacks and gridlock. We know talk is cheap, and we demand *action*.

Backing ideas that are creative, bound in sound reason and logic, will only make you look forward-thinking now, and prescient in the future. And as a young candidate, they can criticize you for your lack of work experience and for your youth, but when you offer alternative solutions to existing problems, they won't be able to criticize you for not having a plan of action.

My hope is that, through the issues I presented on my platform for Syosset Schools, the issues on the platforms of the other young elected officials in this book, and the issues you hear in feedback from your constituents, you'll be able to develop a diverse and comprehensive platform of ideas to attack the problems in your community.

Nicole Malliotakis ran for a totally separate office than I did, representing a totally separate constituency, and therefore had totally separate issues on her platform during her campaign.

Nicole's biggest issue? Dysfunction in New York's capital.

As Nicole mentioned earlier, Albany had just passed the "latest budget in the history of New York." She recalls this dysfunction manifesting in a, "Deficit of $13 Billion, a late budget...other people agreed that the government was not properly representing the people." Nicole took her message of accountable governing, common sense reforms, and responsible spending straight to her constituents, recalling that her campaign, "Had a good message that resonated with people...we worked hard, went door to door, spoke to individuals, explained why I wanted to do this, and explained the ideas I had."

This is a crucial point Nicole raises. Though we will discuss specific strategies surrounding campaigning, like going door-to-door, it's Nicole's tenacity to share her vision for New York with the residents of her community that I emulate, and encourage everyone else to as well. **When you are passionate about your ideas, people notice; the more people you share those ideas with, the more people you are bringing into the fold of your campaign and the stronger traction your campaign will get.**

Personal experience also can yield issues on your platform.

Nicole a Staten Island native, remembers that in 2010, "Eight of my bus lines were eliminated." Flash forward to after her election, and she says that, "We were able to restore most of these since we took office." **Elected officials who keep their campaign promises get rewarded by the voters**; Nicole's been re-elected twice, receiving 73% of the vote in 2014 from Assembly District 64.[55]

For New York State Comptroller Tom DiNapoli, reform in the Mineola, NY, school district became a bipartisan cause.

Though a registered Democrat, Tom joined together with "Mr. Tedone, a registered Conservative" in sharing the "same opinion that parents and students are closed out of decision making." Tom admits that he often disagreed with, "Some of my closest allies, when we spoke about [national] politics...but when it came to school issues we agreed."

---

[55] "Nicole Malliotakis - Ballotpedia." 2013. 15 Nov. 2015 <http://ballotpedia.org/Nicole_Malliotakis>

Additionally, Tom spoke of Larry Egean, a conservative PTA dad, who was also an ally of his. Tom says that you, "Needed people to go to board of education meetings and raise issues," and that Mr. Egean, "Would come to meetings and would reinforce what I was saying, and vice-versa."

Tom's platform focused on making Mineola's school district more inclusive of its residents, and enhancing participation among community stakeholders.

Tom looked to, "Create a budget advisory committee, for students to have a role in issues like textbook selection." Tom foresaw these committees as "not specifically just students, but to allow for broader community involvement"

Another issue Tom sought to reform was the way Mineola handled voting. In Syosset, as it is almost everywhere else on Long Island and in New York State today, residents vote on the same day in May for both the school district budget and for school board of education candidates. However things were run differently in Mineola. Tom says that on Election Day in May you, "Voted for board of education members, but you didn't vote for the budget on school election day...the budget was voted on the night before in a town hall meeting." Regarding voting for the budget, Tom says that there was a budget hearing preceding the vote, and that, "Whoever showed up by the end of the hearing" would vote that night. He continues, "In a modern era, we'd only get 150-200 people to vote at 11:00 p.m." Tom believed, as is nearly universal today, that the budget vote should be on the same day as board members are voted for, and that, "It should be a private vote in a voting machine."

Noting how Mineola was "way behind the times," Mineola voters would later pass a referendum to "open up the system," all leading to "taxpayer interests being better included."

Let's head down south to our favorite West Virginia Mountaineer, Saira Blair. Nicole and I are both New Yorkers who live less than 90 minutes apart, yet even our communities set totally different priorities for us; you can bet that after 5 hours on I-78, you'll wind up in a completely unique community from ours as well. Representing a district in West Virginia, a state with a struggling economy, Saira says the biggest issue on her platform was jobs.

Saira is keenly focused on the employment situation of her constituents; she says that, "Less than 50% of working age adults are actually employed, which is the lowest employment rate in the United States."[56] And it's this calamity that Saira says, "Has a toll on every single other area" of her state. An example of the ripple effects on the jobs crisis? Education.

Saira explains how, "It's hard for students to get a good education if their parents are unemployed...having a good breakfast, getting to school, receiving help with homework at night...good paying jobs help to sew up a lot of problems students are facing."

Saira also focused her platform on energy. She says that, "West Virginia is known as the coal state...I believe that coal keeps the lights on, but our generation will come up with an economically feasible alternative energy with a different type of job in the technology sector." Saira says that she hopes to, "Diversify our industry here in West Virginia to bring in technology jobs, manufacturing jobs...we're not prepared to keep

---

[56] "Unemployment Rates for States - Bureau of Labor Statistics." 2010. 6 Nov. 2015 <http://www.bls.gov/web/laus/laumstrk.htm>

students getting educated in West Virginia jobs to keep them in the state."

Saira's motivation to keep Millennials raised in West Virginia in the state as working adults underscores something special about young elected officials; we often have a different level of motivation than elected officials from previous generations.

You see, for Saira, like for me and for scores of young elected officials throughout the U.S., her job is _personal._ It's personal because the issues she focuses on directly impact her peers. In Saira's case, she has the ability to make a difference in the lives of other West Virginia Millennials—to help keep them in the state she loves. For me, it's ensuring that the Syosset School District is financially sustainable for decades to come, so that the children of my classmates can get the very same quality of education that their parents had. I often get asked by young people considering running for office whether it's possible to make a difference through politics. Whether it's Saira helping young people stay in her state, Nicole restoring transportation lines for her neighbors, or scores of other examples from this book, the answer is simple: absolutely (more on this later).

From West Virginia let's move back north to Millburn, New Jersey, where Chase Harrison's platform was, "Centered completely around student issues." Chase tells me that, "Homework, student mental health, APs [exams], sleep, summer work, school start times, the school calendar, stress, and curriculum were my main issues."

Chase says that he chose to focus his platform around student issues for two reasons: first, "They are the issues I am most passionate about. I feel that these issues are rarely addressed and many have dire effects on the student body." And secondly, "There was no chance any of the other candidates knew as much about these issues as me. By focusing my campaign on these issues, I was able to shift the focus of the election to these issues."

Chase continues that, "At the debates and in media interviews, all candidates were asked about these issues. Obviously, I sounded the smartest on them. The fact that the election became focused on these issues ended up proving to voters that they were critical issues facing the district. Thus, I was the natural choice to deal with them."

He warns young candidates not to adapt their platforms to match the other candidates in the race, but rather to embrace their own expertise in a particular field. He says that, **"One of the biggest mistakes I think young candidates make is choosing issues that don't play to the strengths of being young. Choose issues that highlight why your perspective is necessary. You usually aren't going to beat adults on budget or legal issues."**

This is a brilliant strategy Chase utilized. Think about it—if Jack Lew, current secretary of the treasury, runs for president, he would focus his platform on economic issues because of his expertise in the field; he wouldn't make foreign policy or health care his campaign's primary focus, even if the other candidates did. I strongly endorse Chase's strategy of focusing on what you know most about. Whether you're a small business owner like Brandon Pugh and want to talk about boosting the local economy, or you're a student and want to address student issues like Chase did, it's wise to play to your strengths.

Let's stay in New Jersey, and head 40 minutes west on I-80 to Anthony Fasano in Hopatcong.

Anthony Fasano says that the Hopatcong School District "was in a point of crisis," and this became the focus of his campaign. Anthony believed this crisis stemmed from multiple sources, including the district's "major financial woes...the curriculum wasn't updated...policy and board wise we failed to see it [the crisis]."

Recalling how "students and parents didn't believe in the district," and how "hundreds of students would leave the district to get their public education somewhere else," Anthony summed up the mood in his community as "very frustrated."

Anthony's platform was centered on alleviating these problems he saw in his community, which is politics 101. **Stay close to home with the issues on your platform.** Remember that just last year, House Majority Leader Eric Cantor lost in a primary for re-election to unknown economics professor David Brat because, as many, such as the Dallas Morning News suggested, he "forgot where he came from."[57] Cantor raised $5.7 Million; Brat raised just $231,000.[58] **Your constituents want to see that you are working hard to fight for the issues they care about, and are actively seeking solutions to remedy existing problems facing your community.** As Anthony did, it's important to stay disciplined with a focus on matters at home.

He says that the main issues on his platform, "Were transparency and accountability, financial reform, focusing on encompassing the needs of every

[57] "Editorial: Eric Cantor lost because he forgot where he came ..." 2014. 15 Nov. 2015 <http://www.dallasnews.com/opinion/editorials/20140613-why-eric-cantor-lost.ece>
[58] "David Brat Beats Eric Cantor Despite Raising Just $231,000 ..." 2014. 15 Nov. 2015 <http://www.wsj.com/articles/david-brat-beats-eric-cantor-despite-raising-just-231-000-1402455265>

aspect of the community, whether you're a parent, student, business owner, resident with no children, religious leader...coming together as a community."

Anthony, through NJ Outreach and the myriad of clubs and organizations he was a part of during high school, was a ubiquitous fixture in his community. This allowed him to help bridge relationships between community interest groups and the school district. Anthony is an example of how concepts in this book build upon each other; Anthony decided he wanted to run, understood the impending difficulty of his race, got involved in his community, laid out a plan for action, and through his preparation, was able to achieve success after taking the Oath of Office.

<u>Tips</u>

#1 Share your ideas with as many voters as you can. When you are passionate about your ideas, people notice; the more people you share those ideas with, the more people you are bringing into the fold of your campaign and the stronger traction your campaign will get. For Nicole Malliotakis, it was her tenacity to share her vision for New York with the residents of her community that I emulate, and encourage everyone else to as well.

#2 Focus your platform on what you know most about. Whether you're a small business owner like Brandon Pugh and want to talk about boosting the local economy, or you're a student and want to address student life issues like Chase Harrison did, it's wise to play to your strengths.

#3 Enacting reform on the local level can and should be a bipartisan effort. Take Tom DiNapoli, who this day is heralded by Republicans and Democrats as the consummate public servant; somebody who works with anyone, regardless of their party affiliation, to get the job done.[59] Tom admits that he often disagreed with, "Some of my closest allies, when we spoke about [national] politics...but when it came to school issues we agreed."

#4 Stay close to home with the issues on your platform. Remember that just last year, House Majority Leader Eric Cantor lost in a primary for re-

---

[59] "Dinkins: DiNapoli A Public Servant - Albany Watch Albany ..." 2010. 15 Nov. 2015 <http://statepolitics.lohudblogs.com/2010/10/29/dinkins-dinapoli-a-public-servant/>

election to unknown economics professor David Brat because, as many such as the Dallas Morning News suggest, he "forgot where he came from."[60] Cantor raised $5.7 Million; Brat raised just $231,000.[61] Your constituents want to see that you are working hard to fight for the issues they care about, and are actively seeking solutions to remedy existing problems facing your community. As Anthony Fasano did, it's important to stay disciplined with a focus on matters at home.

[60] "Editorial: Eric Cantor lost because he forgot where he came ..." 2014. 15 Nov. 2015 <http://www.dallasnews.com/opinion/editorials/20140613-why-eric-cantor-lost.ece>

[61] "David Brat Beats Eric Cantor Despite Raising Just $231,000 ..." 2014. 15 Nov. 2015 <http://www.wsj.com/articles/david-brat-beats-eric-cantor-despite-raising-just-231-000-1402455265>

__Chapter Summary__

-Politics is a competition of *ideas*. It's a competition of principles and ideals; a competition of the visions that people have for a community, for a state, or even a country. And the best part about this competition? The judges that decide who wins are your neighbors.

-Your constituents set your priorities. Of course you can have your own ideas on how to improve your community; these ideas may even be contrary to popular belief at the time. But you work for your constituents, and they set the top of your agenda. And the way you figure out what their priorities are is by talking to them *before* you run.

-Backing ideas that are creative, bound in sound reason and logic, will only make you look forward-thinking now, and prescient in the future. And as a young candidate, they can criticize you for your lack of work experience and for your youth, but when you offer alternative solutions to existing problems, they won't be able to criticize you for not having a plan of action.

-For Millennials who serve, like it is for Saira Blair, for me and for scores of young elected officials throughout the U.S., the job is *personal*. It's personal because the issues we focus on often directly impact our peers. I often get asked by young people considering running for office whether it's possible to make a difference through politics. Whether it's Saira helping young people stay in her state, Nicole restoring transportation lines for her neighbors, or scores of other examples from this book, the answer is simple: absolutely.

The Campaign

Marie Lu, author of the futuristic dystopian "Legend" series wrote that, "If you want to rebel, rebel from inside the system. That's much more powerful than rebelling outside the system."[62] While the campaigns you will run are set in modern-day America, I agree with Lu's mantra that it is far more effective to rebel from inside the system than outside.

Having said this, I do want to make clear my belief that action from outside the system is paramount to making change as well; looking for ways to make your community, your state, and your country better is patriotic. And almost all of the great social movements in this country have had youth at their core. With all the darkness in the world today—the ubiquitousness of terror and violence and hate—I heed the words of Robert F. Kennedy Jr.:

"This world demands the qualities of youth: not a time of life but a state of mind, a temper of the will, a quality of imagination, a predominance of courage over timidity, of the appetite for adventure over the love of ease."[63]

This country, this world, is the one *we* will inherit. So we can either get off the sidelines and check

[62] "Quotes About Revolution (732 quotes) - Goodreads." 2011. 16 Nov. 2015 <http://www.goodreads.com/quotes/tag/revolution>
[63] "Quotations to Inspire Youth Power - The Freechild Project." 2004. 16 Nov. 2015 <http://www.freechild.org/quotations.htm>

into the game, or sit back and spectate. The young elected officials in this book have made their choices clear—my greatest hope is that you'll join them.

But even with the need for youth to rebel from the outside by getting involved in nonprofit organizations and social movements, the greatest need for youth is *in* the government.

Our voices simply are not being heard; and in my life, I have found no better way to make our voices heard, and to make real and meaningful change in our communities, than by serving in elected office.

What's the significance of all of this? If you're going to rebel from inside the system, you have to first *win* your election.

And as you know from reading this book, it's a difficult task.

Worse is that unfortunately politicians in America with the best ideas, with the most passion, who would make the best representatives, do not always win.

The best candidates are the ones who make their campaigns their *own*; they take a little from everyone, but they put their own unique twist on their campaign. You will find yourself agreeing with many of the ideas expressed in this chapter, and you may disagree with some of the approaches that others, including myself, took during our campaigns. That's okay! The beauty of this book is to take what you like and leave what you don't like—that hand-in-the-sand mentality that my brother Justin spoke of.

This book aims to give you all the tools to be successful on Election Day, and this chapter will be a holistic, 360-degree view of the campaign process. We'll start with the importance of believing in your campaign, talk about deadlines and documents, knocking on doors and making phone calls, and everything else in between all the way through to Election Night.

Belief in Your Campaign

Miley Cyrus, formerly known as Hannah Montana, once prophesized that, "If you believe in yourself, anything is possible."[64] When it comes to campaigning, she's absolutely right.

Look at every young elected official in this book; each one achieved something great because they believed in their campaigns, and this was a crucial factor in their victories.

The first step in campaigning is deciding right here, right now, that you believe you *can* win. Despite your doubters, despite your detractors, despite every single medium of negative energy in the world pointed your way, you have to believe that you can do this. And as was mentioned before, many times during your campaign this belief will be tested. This is precisely why you need to make a powerful commitment to yourself that you will not lose faith *before* the process begins.

Here's a crucial lesson I learned about campaigns; it doesn't matter what the polls or the pundits say. If you don't believe, with all your heart, that you can win, you're not going to convince anybody to vote for you.

Remember that the majority of young elected officials in this book, including myself, were major underdogs for the entirety of our races.

---

[64] "If you believe in yourself anything is possible. - BrainyQuote." 16 Nov. 2015
<http://www.brainyquote.com/quotes/quotes/m/mileycyrus409344.html>

Take Ellen Nesbitt. Ellen was a huge underdog in her race for Dutchess County Legislator, running as a Republican in a district with a Democratic to Republican enrollment ratio of 3:1. The doubt surrounding her candidacy was immense; even her own family members were hesitant about her running for that seat. And those serving in the legislature at the time? Ellen recalls how, "Nobody in the legislature thought we were going to win." It was Ellen's unwavering belief in herself and her campaign, her outlook to ignore the numbers and just focus on the people, and her "won't quit attitude" that carried her to be elected and re-elected. It's this attitude that I advise each young candidate to adopt during his or her race.

For me, my belief in myself and my candidacy was sustained by my family. As I mentioned in the Introduction, my own best friends told me that, "I was following, "The worst life plan ever," and that, "I would regret this mistake for the rest of my life."
Motivational speaker Jim Rohn believes that we are the average of the five people we spend the most time with.[65] It was during my campaign that I switched friend groups, and started to keep a smaller circle. To this day, I continually re-evaluate who the people in my life are that I want to remain close with. Because campaigns are hard. They're an emotional ordeal, and incredibly difficult on their own; when you have people in your life filling your head with negativity and bringing you down, they become borderline impossible to be with. **That is why I advise you to heed Rohn's guidance and surround yourself with only those people who will make you the**

---

[65] "Jim Rohn: You're The Average Of The Five People You ..." 2012. 16 Nov. 2015 <http://www.businessinsider.com/jim-rohn-youre-the-average-of-the-five-people-you-spend-the-most-time-with-2012-7>

very best version of yourself. Of course you should not surround yourself with a bunch of "yes men" who don't offer any contrary opinions ever. But to believe in yourself, and be the very best candidate you can be, you should surround yourself with those who will *encourage* rather than *discourage,* and pick you up when you're down. For me, that's my family. For some, it's their friends or teammates. For others, it's a significant other. Regardless of who it is, as discussed during the segment about your support system, it's invaluable to your campaign.

Slogan & Branding

Yes, you may have thought slogans were only a thing when you ran for treasurer of your fourth grade class. (Unfortunately I had to scrap my plans for *Get Off Your Can, Vote for Lafazan!* because my mother found it too "risqué.") Well slogans are an important part of politics regardless of the office you seek, from Senator John McCain's *Country First,* to Governor Chris Christie's *Telling It Like It Is,* to President Barack Obama's *Yes We Can.*

For your campaign, a slogan is all about branding as it's often the first thing a voter notices when you hand them a piece of literature, or when they browse your website (we'll cover all of this). **I encourage you to choose a slogan that will brand you as both the type of candidate you want to be portrayed as, and the type of elected official you want to be known as.** Your slogan can stick with you forever, or it can change from race to race. You only get one, so think long and hard about what you want it to be.

For example, take Ian Calderon. His slogan? *New Ideas. Fresh Perspective.* It's bolded on the top of his website.[66] It's used in his press releases.[67] It's everywhere.

This is textbook political branding.

As one of the youngest members of the California State Assembly, Ian wanted to be seen as a leader of the next generation, who rather than recycling old and tired ideas will bring creative ideas and a new outlook to the office he holds.

Take Saira Blair. Her slogan for her race for the West Virginia House of Delegates was: *A Voice for Working West Virginians*. Voters knew up front where her priorities would lie; with the working class. She says that, **"I wanted to show I was the candidate to give a voice to the voiceless. Too many West Virginians were falling out of the middle class and leaving the state. I wanted to make sure people knew I would fight for every resident, and not just the connected."**

Take Connor Kurtz from Pennsylvania. His campaign slogan was quite simple and to the point— *Working Hard For Local Families*.[68] It's right up on the top banner of this website. And this slogan is perfect for Connor. With a keen focus on property taxes, serving on the Daniel Boone Area Board of Directors is just that— working hard for the local families of his community.

---

[66] "Ian Calderon for Assembly District 57." 2013. 16 Nov. 2015 <http://www.ianccalderon.com/>

[67] "Ian Calderon Takes Oath as New Assemblymember for 57th ..." 2012. 16 Nov. 2015 <http://asmdc.org/members/a57/news-room/press-releases/ian-calderon-takes-oath-as-new-assemblymember-for-57th-district>

[68] "Connor Kurtz - School Director for Amity Township." 2011. 16 Nov. 2015 <http://schoolboard.connorkurtz.org/>

Joshua A. Lafazan

My slogan? *A Fresh Voice For The 21st Century.*[69] I chose this slogan because I felt a main problem with the incumbents on the school board was that they were not forward thinking. They weren't looking at which tools students needed to compete in a complex 21st century economy. They weren't looking to protect the school district's financial position for the next generation of Syosset students. And there were certainly no fresh ideas coming from any of the members of the board, because there was no public discussion or debate at the board meetings! I've kept this slogan, and it's right at the top of my blog, because to this day I work hard to be that fresh voice for my constituents, and I'm always looking at whether we, as a community, are doing the best job of preparing our graduates for the future.

Slogans are just as important for when you hold office as when you're campaigning for office.

Take Daniel Zolnikov from Montana. If you go to Daniel's Facebook page, he's described as a "Young, Liberty Minded, Conservative Montana State Representative of House District 45 in Billings."[70] For Daniel, this statement is all about the type of representative he is. He was heralded by *Forbes* for his push for privacy bills and protecting journalistic sources. His conservative credentials were acknowledged by *Red Alert Politics*, and, being from a small town in Montana, he never forgets who he represents and where he came from.[71]

---

[69] "A Fresh Voice for the 21st Century." 2012. 16 Nov. 2015 <http://joshlafazan.blogspot.com/>

[70] "Daniel Zolnikov - Facebook." 2013. 16 Nov. 2015 <https://www.facebook.com/DanielZolnikov/>

[71] "Daniel Zolnikov - Red Alert Politics." 2015. 16 Nov. 2015 <http://redalertpolitics.com/thirty-under-thirty-2014/daniel-zolnikov/>

Take Anthony Fasano from New Jersey. His slogan is: *Moving Forward, Together*. In a blog post to the Hopatcong community, Anthony wrote that, "2015 has to be the year that we inform the uninformed, who are misinformed, about what being a part of the Hopatcong Borough School District really means. That responsibility starts with me."[72] Remember that when Anthony took office, he says that Hopatcong School District was, "In a point of crisis." So Anthony wanted to make one thing clear with his slogan; that he would be the representative that would bring everyone together. He wanted to stress inclusivity, as well as the need for progress; his slogan accomplished both.

Take Nicole Malliotakis from Staten Island, New York. Her slogan is just two words: "Our Assemblywoman."[73] Almost all politicians (except some currently seeking the office of the U.S. Presidency) want to be seen as bipartisan. For Nicole, it's genuine. As *Observer News* reported:

> "Democratic State Senator Diane Savino and Republican Assemblywoman [Malliotakis] both get along extremely well, and their Staten Island-based districts even overlap. According to the *Staten Island Advance*, both Ms. Savino and Ms. Malliotakis shop together at the same Staten Island Mall Macy's, arrive together at many of

---

[72] "Moving Forward, Together." 2013. 16 Nov. 2015 <http://ajfasano.blogspot.com/>
[73] "Nicole Malliotakis for New York State Assembly." 2010. 16 Nov. 2015 <http://nicolemalliotakis.com/>

the same political events and drive up to Albany together as well."[74]

For Nicole, her slogan stresses that her position is about getting the job done, whether you're a Republican, Democrat or Independent living in her district. And that's exactly the type of representative she is; above partisanship, and wholeheartedly for the people.

Documents and Deadlines

Deadlines, deadlines, deadlines! There will be several deadlines which you must meet during the span of your campaign. Unlike a deadline for a paper which a teacher can move back, these deadlines are non-negotiable. Don't take yourself out of the race for silly negligence.

Every elected official in this book had to collect signatures on a nominating petition and had to file that petition by a certain date to become candidates on the ballot. The amount of signatures required varies by the size of the office you seek; for example, a county legislator representing 100,000 people needs more signatures than a town councilman representing 25,000, and so on. But don't worry; instructions on how many signatures you need, and who counts as a signatory, will be listed on this petition. For example, in a nonpartisan election, like my race for the Syosset School Board, any qualified voter over the age of 18 who lived in the Syosset School District area counted. But if your race is partisan, you may only be able to receive

[74] "Diane Savino and Nicole Malliotakis: Bipartisan BFFs - New ..." 2014. 16 Nov. 2015 <http://observer.com/2012/01/diane-savino-and-nicole-malliotakis-bipartisan-bffs/>

signatures from qualified voters registered in your party.

Some very important notes regarding nominating petitions:

-Find out when those deadlines are now! Call the clerk's office for your school district, your town or county, or the board of elections. Mark these dates down, and do not wait for the last minute; gathering enough signatures takes far more time than you will originally anticipate.

-If you get stuck, and cannot gain access to this information, you can always submit a FOIL request with your municipality. A FOIL request "allows members of the public to access records of governmental agencies."[75]

-Do NOT falsify your petitions. Of course, the reason you should not falsify your petitions is because we are a new and ethical generation of leaders. But as many don't know, falsifying a petition is illegal. David Denenberg, a former Nassau County Legislator, pleaded guilty to a misdemeanor in 2005 for falsifying a petition.[76]

-Whatever the minimum number of required signatures, collect more. Some voters may not be registered, some may not live in your district, and

[75] "FOIL - New York State Education Department." 2014. 19 Nov. 2015 <http://www.nysed.gov/foil>

[76] "Legislator Pleads Guilty To Falsifying a Petition - NYTimes ..." 2008. 18 Nov. 2015 <http://query.nytimes.com/gst/fullpage.html?res=9C04E4DB1638F931A 25752C0A9639C8B63>

for a host of other reasons, some of your signatures may be thrown out. That is why, through extra effort, you protect yourself from ballot invalidation.

How do you get these signatures?

I found that knocking on doors was a great way to gather signatures; you're speaking to voters as it is, so ask them for their signature in addition to giving them a piece of literature. If your election in nonpartisan, you can knock on any home to gather a signature; if your election is partisan, you're going to want to knock on the doors of registered voters in your party. You can receive this information from your county's board of elections.

Another strategy is to ask your volunteers to help you collect signatures (read the instructions on top of your petition and make sure this is allowed). For my race in 2012, I was able to meet my minimum quota of signatures faster than anticipated by having 10 friends complete a sheet of 13 signatures each. Remember, campaigns are a team effort.

Additionally, each candidate had to submit multiple financial disclosure forms. These reports detail how much money you raise, who donated to your campaigns, etc. When you file your signatures with the clerk or Board of Elections for your municipality, you will receive these documents.

Next, you most likely will receive questionnaires from media outlets, either from your municipality or directly from them. Be mindful of these deadlines as well! Your answers to these questions are important as to some voters this will be your one and only introduction; take care of this right away!

Despite the pressing nature of these deadlines, many young elected officials interviewed for this book found this process to be very manageable.

Jon Fiore, from the New York Mills School District, said that, "Deadlines were really no issue to me; being a student at the time, I was quite familiar with attempting to comply with them. Gathering signatures was surprisingly simple as well; I needed to only walk half way up my street and I had gathered all the signatures I required."

Mark Kremer agrees. For Mark, from Southgate Michigan, he touted his organizational skills as being an asset to his campaign. He shared that, "The deadlines were not a problem for me. I am a very organized person when it comes to deadlines."

In fact, Chris Scales, elected in 2014 to the Hamilton Township School Board, even found the process to be memorable. He agrees that, "The major deadline is gathering the necessary signatures to be placed on the ballot." Yet for Chris, "The required amount [of signatures] for school board candidates in New Jersey is 10." I am guessing that your municipality will most likely require more signatures than this; for my re-election this past May, I had to collect 70 signatures. Chris was proactive in ensuring his eligibility to run for his school board, noting, "I had conversations with my County Clerk in November of 2013 about my candidacy, and if I would be able to qualify to be on the ballot. After she gave me the okay, I would wait and wait until the clerk's office posted the application online. As soon as I got it, I went to a community organization's club and expressed my interest in running."

The reception Chris received from this community organization? Nothing short of stellar. They "were all thrilled, but upset that I did not bring additional petitions. I ended up running out of room for people to sign." For Chris, it was also a family affair. He recalls how, "My grandfather and I walked up the steps of the county clerk's office in Trenton, New Jersey, on June 4th, and presented my petition. It was a feeling of great joy, and a moment that I will never forget. I was glad to have my grandfather by my side during this key event in my young life."

Press

As you will speak to scores of people during the exploratory portion of your campaign, you will certainly generate a buzz about your campaign in your community. People talk, and this natural buzz is more advantageous than any press you can get. However this being said, press is a crucial part of any race as it brings many more people into your campaign. Without the press, I wouldn't have won my race (more to come on this).

Aside from Hollywood and Major League Sports, politics is as publicized a profession as there is. It's important to understand that should you choose to run, more likely than not, you're going to get some press.

Local papers are the lifeblood of local politics; though many say print journalism is "dead," I've found it commonplace that residents learned about my candidacy from the local papers. In fact, I even announced my intentions to seek a seat on the school board in an op-ed in my town's local paper, *The Syosset-Jericho Tribune!*[77] This may be something that you want to consider as well.

I found, too, that when you are a first time candidate in a small town, you may have to drum up

---

[77] "Joshua Lafazan Running for Syosset School Board." 2012. 18 Nov. 2015 <http://www.antonnews.com/syossetjerichotribune/news/20609-joshua-lafazan-running-for-syosset-school-board.html>

your own press coverage at first. Reach out to the local papers; let them know who you are, what you're running for, and why you're running. Start small, and work your way up.

After a few articles in the *Syosset Patch*, a hyper-local news organization from AOL, along with my op-ed in the *Syosset-Jericho Tribune*, I then reached out to the bigger publications. *Newsday* is de facto Long Island's newspaper. I called and emailed reporters, letting them know about who I was, and the significance of my race to bring open government and transparency to Syosset. **You see, here's a key distinction; you without a doubt have to be your biggest advocate. However, there's a dichotomy between giving reporters information about your story, and hounding them to cover it. All** too often, the journalists I speak with say they become annoyed when young candidates ask them to cover their story, and then repeatedly ask.

A simple email will suffice:

Dear Ms. Smith,

My name is Joshua Lafazan. As the 18-year-old senior class president at Syosset High School, this May I hope to become one of the youngest elected officials in New York as I am seeking a seat on the Syosset School Board of Education. I feel that Syosset needs to become more transparent and open in the way the district functions, and I believe our community can't wait any longer for change. To learn more about my platform and ideas, please feel free to check out my story in the Syosset Jericho Tribune (insert link). Thanks so much for your time.

With appreciation,

Joshua Lafazan

It's important to note I learned early on, as I shared with you in Chapter 3, that asking for a favor, especially from someone you don't know, will most often not yield the result you want. I advise to simply give reporters information; if they want to cover the story, they will reach out to you.

From my local stories came a story in *Newsday.*[78] And it was this *Newsday* article which landed me an interview on Stuart Varney's show on FOX Business Network.[79] Be patient, the coverage will come. Focus on the things you can control; how hard you work, how well you plan, and how you handle your team of volunteers.

Brain Trust

Steve Jobs, in an interview by the Santa Clara Valley Historical Association, professed that, "Now, I've actually always found something to be very true, which is most people don't get those experiences because they never ask. I've never found anybody who didn't want to help me when I've asked them for help."[80]

---

[78] Syosset class prez seeks school board seat | Newsday." 2012. 18 Nov. 2015 <http://www.newsday.com/long-island/nassau/syosset-class-prez-seeks-school-board-seat-1.3688221>

[79] "School District Head Paid $540K While Freezing Teachers ..." 2012. 18 Nov. 2015 <http://video.foxbusiness.com/v/1619486568001/school-district-head-paid-540k-while-freezing-teachers-pay/>

[80] "Steve Jobs on the Remarkable Power of Asking for ... - Inc.com." 2015. 18 Nov. 2015 <http://www.inc.com/peter-economy/steve-jobs-on-the-remarkable-power-of-asking-for-what-you-want.html>

One of biggest mistakes I find young people making during their campaigns is not soliciting enough advice. We don't have a great deal of life experience yet, and there's nothing we can do about it. However, the way we make up for this is by soliciting advice from those who do have life experience.

Equally as important, we must solicit advice from people in the specific area of expertise in which we wish to serve. If you're running for a seat on the school board, it's incumbent upon you to speak to teachers, parents, administrators, and other community stakeholders. If you're running for mayor, it's incumbent upon you to speak to police officers, firefighters, city council members, etc. As Cyrus Habib said in Chapter 3, "Dress for the job you want to have." Speak with all those people who you will serve and interact with, and who have institutional knowledge that you may benefit from.

My younger brother Justin has a great quote about which people to seek advice from. He says to, "Reverse-engineer the process with your own special twist. Collaborate with others in and out of your industry or field, and work to seek mutually beneficial outcomes."[81]

So, you want to run for a specific office; find people who currently hold or previously held that office! Again, adults do enjoy helping motivated Millennials. Contact information for every elected official is listed online, and those interviewed in this book have contact information listed at the end. Reach out, let them know you are running, and ask for

---

[81] "Mantra — Justin Lafazan." 2015. 18 Nov. 2015
<http://www.justinlafazan.com/mantra/>

mentorship. This worked for me, and I promise it will work for you.

But it's not just politicos who I take advice from; I have a diverse group of people who mentor me, and I call them my "brain trust." The term "brain trust" was originally coined by James Kieran, a *New York Times* reporter, referring, "To the group of academic advisers that FDR gathered to assist him during the 1932 presidential campaign."[82] I seek advice from those in business, law, finance, energy, education, and many more fields; expose yourself to a collection of differing expertises and opinions, and you will only grow both as a thinker and a leader.

Your brain trust will be invaluable to you. There will come a time when you serve in which a topic will come up that you have limited knowledge about. These are the times when you'll be thankful you have a rolodex to summon and committed people who care about you to help you.

Campaign Team

It's often said that there's no "I" in team. Well there are two "I's" in politics, and it projects the unbelievable level of arrogance some elected officials have today. Candidates receive votes, but races are won and lost by their campaign teams. Whether you're running for student council secretary or for the United States Senate, the people you have behind you will either

---

[82] "FDR's Brains Trust - The George Washington University." 2015. 18 Nov. 2015 <https://www.gwu.edu/~erpapers/teachinger/glossary/brains-trust.cfm>

propel you to victory, or lose the race long before it's officially over.

I want to make this clear; without my campaign team, my friends who spent countless hours assisting me during my campaign, from late nights and frigid mornings, I wouldn't have won my race. These people are the core foundation of your campaign.

For Anthony Fasano, he similarly gives credit where credit is due–his team. He tells me that, "I wouldn't have gotten where I am without their help...most of our success came from people on the team with new ideas."

Additionally, you want campaign volunteers helping you because your campaign should be as inclusive as possible. Some people you don't know personally may reach out and ask to help–absolutely let them! Do not be so arrogant as to believe you can do this all on your own. It's the kiss of death for young candidates. If residents want to put up signs, if they want to make phone calls, if they want to distribute literature, graciously accept their help. I would've gotten my ass kicked without them (I promised I'd only curse one time, mom!).

So how do you find a campaign team? Anthony Fasano says that, "The first thing I did was I took all of my old classmates and high school friends and I brought them together in the winter of 2013," telling them, "I need your help to be part of my team." A former athlete in high school, Anthony knows all too well about the importance of teamwork. His campaign team consisted of members ranging from "ages 16 to 68." Anthony's campaign was a perfect example of inclusivity of everybody, from every corner of his community.

He recalls how some on his team, "Did promotions, some did innovation, some did strategy, some did social media, some did press relations...each member had specific jobs they took very seriously."

This is a lesson in leadership for everyone—in order to have the best team possible, your volunteers have to buy into your campaign. **I've volunteered on campaigns before where I felt valueless, and I've helped candidates who always went out of their way to make me feel valued. You can imagine which candidates I worked harder for.**

For me, the first step was finding a campaign manager.

My favorite television show of all time is *The West Wing* (every college student has at one point or another succumbed to a Netflix binge—this was mine). In episode 12 of season 1, President Bartlet taps Secretary of Agriculture Roger Tribbey to be the "designated survivor," the person from the president's cabinet who does not attend the State of the Union in case tragedy strikes. In good spirits President Bartlet gives Secretary Tribbey instructions to take in case such tragedy did occur, such as moving the military to DEFCON 4. President Bartlet then asks Secretary Tribbey if he has a best friend. He replies yes. President Bartlet asks, "Is he smarter than you?" He again replies yes. President Bartlet follows up with, "Would you trust him with your life. Once more, he says yes." President Bartlet smiles and says, "That's your chief of staff."

For most politicians, their campaign managers turn into their chief of staff, as these positions require incredible trust, loyalty, and competence.

So for me, the choice of campaign manager was made easy for me; it would be one of my best friends in the world, Myles Blodnick.

I'd always respected Myles for his superb intellect. As we speak, Myles is the president of the Carnegie Mellon Debate Team, where he'll earn a degree in artificial intelligence in May of 2016. But it was Myles' heart that put me at ease; I knew that no matter what, no matter how much we disagreed, he always had my best interests at heart. That was invaluable to me, and was precisely what made us a formidable team.

So why did Myles decide to come along for the crazy ride that was my campaign? He loves to tell the story:

> "I originally decided to help out Josh with his campaign when we were attending a Harvard Debate tournament invitational while in high school. A few members of the team and I were grabbing dinner at Mr. Bartley's, a famous local burger joint, after a day of debates. Somehow the conversation became steered from basketball to girls to school. That's when Josh went off. He listed the best things about our high school, but also the things that needed improvement. He was suggesting viable solutions, but everyone just seemed to shrug them off, assuming that the "adults" would have done it by now if it made sense. Josh then told us about how he would run for the school board and make those changes. Almost everyone laughed. I had never seen someone so passionate about how Syosset could be better. I decided then, if Josh was serious, I would do whatever it took to help him out."

You see, it's interesting—what the world got to see of my campaign was the shiny ending: the press conferences, the television appearances, the celebrations. **What the world didn't see was the long nights in my basement brainstorming. The early mornings at the train station handing out literature. The 5 minute dinners in between campaign events.** And for each one of these memories, there's one person who was always by my side—Myles. Similar to having a workout partner at the gym to keep you motivated, your campaign manager is that person who will keep you going for the entirety of your campaign, from dusk until dawn, Monday through Sunday.

So while Myles and I eventually achieved success, pulling off what we believed to be one of the biggest political upsets in the country, boy was it a long, arduous, and exhausting process. Myles recalls that:

> "Being a campaign manager is difficult. Being a campaign manager for a high school student is a pain in the ass. As Josh's campaign manager, I had to help recruit volunteers, constantly try to brand and define our campaign and its message, and deal with many daily tasks. Trying to get national media coverage for a local school board election was difficult, but anything can get done if you relentlessly call news sources. How else would Josh end up being reported in the New York Post? However, the most important thing a campaign manager can do is lead by example. I knocked on every door in my neighborhood at least twice, and got doors slammed in my face almost as many times, had to publicly debate people who felt Josh was unqualified, and spent my Saturdays campaigning outside supermarkets."

Your campaign will only achieve success if you're willing to sacrifice for it (we'll cover this more soon). But be cognizant that you're not the only one who will sacrifice. **Remember, candidates receive votes, but races are won and lost by their campaign teams.**

Additionally, like Anthony, my team was an eclectic group of people. I went to all the different types of students in my high school to ask for help. And here's the key to getting a lot of help; the majority of people will not be able to contribute a great deal of time. High school and college students are super busy, and have multiple obligations after class. But this isn't an issue, because getting a large group of people to volunteer sporadically instead is incredibly effective. Have friend groups of 5-10 people volunteer together, whether it's making phone calls for a few hours or knocking on doors in a neighborhood. They'll enjoy working together with their friends, and you'll be able to amass the most help possible.

I advise to start with your closest friends; they will be most motivated to help you (and often you will often be able to guilt them into helping you by virtue of them owing you favors over the years!).

Take my buddies Jake Asman and Dan Budick. Jake and Dan and now juniors majoring in journalism at the Roy H. Park School of Communications at Ithaca College. Jake and Dan call the football games for the Ithaca Bombers, and host their own sports radio show with featured guests such as Buster Olney and Kevin Harlan—nothing to do with politics.[83] Yet when I

---

[83] "Interview w/ Kevin Harlan | The Asman and Budick ... - ICTV." 2015. 20 Nov. 2015 <http://ictv.org/asmanandbudick/412/>

approached them to help me with my campaign, they didn't hesitate. Jake says that he joined the campaign, "Because I believed in Josh's platform for fresh ideas from a young person's perspective. Syosset needed a change and I felt that Josh was the right person to help lead Syosset in the right direction. I believed that Josh will always do what is right for the Syosset community." And Dan says that, "I believed in Josh's message because I saw the corruption in the district. I saw that our tax money wasn't being used in the way it should to better not only our district but our community. I believed with Josh on the board that he would not only improve the district, but the lives of the individuals who call Syosset home."

It doesn't matter if your friends are die-hard politicos, or sports junkies like mine; your real friends will have your back when you come asking for help.

My campaign in 2012 was unique because it was run exclusively by young people. But that was not to say that adults didn't play a huge role—be inclusive of everybody and anybody who wants to help you.

Internships for high school students are also a great way to get motivated young people involved in your campaigns. High school students are in need of community service and experiences to put on their resumes for college. So rather than working in the district office for a congressman making phone calls or sending letters, you can offer a much more compelling and personal experience. Whereas interns see a congressman maybe once during their entire internship, your interns can work directly with you every day, and gain a much better insight into grassroots campaigning and local politics. Major thank you to the interns who were so amazing on my re-election campaign: Andrew Feldman, Aaron Kaplan,

Evan Lubash, Lance Lustig, Austin Golove, Austen Yan, and Sean Leyden.

Youth IS our advantage to achieve the impossible, and Millennials will be your secret weapon in your campaigns. Heed Myles' advice when he says, "The youth are a necessity in any successful campaign today. There is no other demographic more informed due to their constant sharing of information. They know how to best spread the word and utilize technology in their favor, which is now critical in a modern campaign."

Knocking on Doors

In October of my senior year of high school, my friends and I went to listen to author Michael Moore speak at The Book Revue in Huntington, NY.[84] The reason (aside from an excuse to grab Little Vincent's Pizza in Huntington afterwards) was because at 18, Michael Moore was elected to his school board.[85]

When Michael was done speaking to the audience, he asked if there were any questions; my hand shot up like Apollo 11. In a room crowded like a Manhattan subway during rush hour, I spoke up and nervously said, "Mr. Moore, My name is Josh and at 18, I'm running for my town's school board of education. What's the one piece of advice you have for me?" Michael smiled, thought about it for a second, and

---

[84] "Michael Moore at Book Revue | Huntington, NY Patch." 2014. 18 Nov. 2015 <http://patch.com/new-york/huntington/ev--michael-moore-at-book-revue>

[85] "10 Things You Might Not Know About Michael Moore ..." 2010. 18 Nov. 2015 <http://articles.chicagotribune.com/2007-07-01/news/0706300500_1_michael-moore-rolling-stone-president-bush>

replied, **"Knock on every door in your town. And when you're done? Knock on them again."**

This piece of advice turned into my campaign's mantra; we would knock on every single door that we could, and when we were done, we would do it all over again.

Anthony Fasano follows this ideology. He says that, "My motto was, 'Face-to-face will win the race.'"

I couldn't agree more with Anthony. Local politics is all about that personal connection. Look at Brandon Pugh.

Remember that Brandon, who, "Knocked on 6,000 homes," says that, "A lot of time people can't name any of the current serving board of education members, so as a candidate the most important thing you can do is tell people who you are and what you stand for."

I've found Brandon's assessment to be correct. When voters go to the booth, often they won't know any of all the candidates running for local offices like the school board. But as Brandon says, if you knock on somebody's door, tell them about yourself, why you're running, and what you stand for, you give yourself the best chance of earning that person's vote.

Unlike a presidential race, people in your community know you personally. The more allies you recruit on at the grassroots level, and the more people you speak with who resonate with your message, the better chance you have of winning.

So we've covered why it's important to knock on doors—now let's talk logistics.

Where to knock?

I've found the best places to knock are the places in your community where houses are closest together.

This way, you spend less time walking between houses and more time speaking with voters. For those places where the houses are farther apart, it may be advantageous to have a friend or parent accompany your volunteers with a car. It's quite helpful to plan where you are knocking before you head out. Take Daniel Croson for example.

Daniel says that, **"My running mates and I had a giant campaign map, and we would highlight the streets when we walked them."** The result? They, "Literally knocked on every door" in their community. Daniel recalls that he actually, "Wore a hole in my shoes from so much door walking," and that, "My calves were in really great shape." See? Who needs a gym when you can just run for office! I highly encourage you to adopt Daniel's strategy of strategically planning where you knock, and keeping track of the streets you've covered.

Before you knock, or send your volunteers out to go knock, you can go on *Google Maps* and look up the street names in specific neighborhoods you want to cover. By assigning people streets to complete rather than individual neighborhoods, you are helping to avoid confusion and are staying organized; as Daniel did, you should absolutely keep track of which streets you completed.

Organization now will, without a doubt, save you time later. Organization also plays a part in keeping track of the responses of voters. As mentioned before, voters will invariably like you, and dislike you. While this is totally normal, this data is *crucial*; it shows you where to allocate your time. Take Tom DiNapoli.

When asked how he went about campaigning, Tom said that his campaign did it, "Very much the old fashioned way...to maximize outreach." He says the, "Real effort was going door-to-door. We had 50-70 students who divvied up the school district and literally covered every block, introducing me, and reminding people when Election Day was." Here's where Tom's campaign excelled in organization; they kept track of voter data. **Tom says that when his volunteers knocked on doors they, "Kept very simple coding for me...favorable, against me, unfavorable, or open minded."**

So when you're knocking on a door and a voter says, "He's already got my vote," you put them in the *favorable* category. When you knock on a door and the voter says, "I'll never vote for him," that's the *against me* category. If the resident says, "I don't love the ideas on his platform," that's *unfavorable*. And if the voter says, "I'd like to learn more about him," that's *open minded*.

It's your campaign; you can make your own rubric for voters with your own categories. But at the end of the day, you need to spend your time getting your *favorable* voters out to the polls, and getting your *open minded* voters more information about you and your ideas. Tom says that on, "March 17, I announced I was running...by the end of campaign I had lists" to work off. Tom did this in under two months; with planning and preparation, you can absolutely do this too. Tom recalls how, "A couple of days before the election we got reverse phone book directories, car pools for people who needed rides...it was a rainy day on May 3, so everything was directed towards having an effective poll operation... **we were surgical in identifying voters.** This type of attitude–a "surgical" approach to identifying voters–is a winning methodology. Because elections come down to turnout; if your campaign can identify those *favorable* voters who make up your support base, persuade those *open minded* voters to vote for you, and bring both of these groups down to the polls, you put yourself in the best position to win.

What to say?

Knocking on a voter's door is far different than giving a speech. In a speech, you have a lot of time to introduce yourself, make solid arguments, provide data, and make a conclusion. With a voter, you most often have 1-2 minutes to make your point; this is what Michaelle Solages calls an "elevator speech."

Michaelle says that, "It takes a lot of groundwork to talk to individuals," as her campaign, "Knocked on thousands and thousands of doors." This is something she, "Recommends to every single young person." Michaelle recalls how she, "Would knock on a door, have to make a two minute elevator speech, and only have their attention for really one minute." The reactions from voters would definitely differ–"I would knock on the door, and after I finished my speech the person would look at me and say wow, either you're young, or a woman, or you had me as soon as you told me you're running for office." Either way, this was a positive reception for Michaelle, whose campaign dominated the "ground game" in her community.

Here's a template for your elevator speech that you cannot go wrong with.

Good evening!

My name is Joshua Lafazan, and I'm running for the Syosset School Board of Education. I'm the senior class president at Syosset High School, and if elected, I'll become one of the youngest elected officials in New York State.

Here is a piece of campaign literature which details my plans for the district. I'm running for the Syosset School Board because I believe we need to be more open and transparent, I believe we need to be aggressive in our actions to slow the rise of property taxes, and I believe our superintendent should not make more money than the president of the United States.

Please feel free to contact me if you'd like to further discuss a specific issue related to the district, or hear more about why I'm running. I hope to earn your support this May 19th at the polls.

Most voters will smile and say thank you, and take your piece of literature inside with them. You will encounter some residents who will treat you with disrespect; I'll never forget the woman who slammed the door in my face in April during my campaign. Remember that "stomach of steel" we have—just shake it off and move on. And there will be some voters who will ask you a few questions on the spot, or want to talk a little further. This is great, but underscores Chase Harrison's point earlier that preparation is key; **you need to know your platform frontwards and backwards.** Additionally, you need to be caught up with current events pertaining to the office you're running for. It was commonplace during my re-election this past May to get asked about actions the New York Board of Regents took, or what Governor Cuomo said in a recent press conference, etc....

What to wear?

This is an area where I find myself in disagreement with my friends who hold political office. To this day, others continue to make my age an issue. Just this year, an older gentleman was condescending to an idea I posed, telling me I hadn't "been around the block" yet. I bit my tongue; as George Carlin remarked, **"Never argue with an idiot. They will only bring you down to their level and beat you with experience."**[86] But I digress. So when I was 16, I decided that no matter where I went I would always be wearing a shirt and tie. Yes, my friend Jon Camposa quips that I look like a used car salesman. But this way, even though I clearly would still look the youngest (I've yet to participate in *No Shave November* as I still can't grow facial hair), I would always look as professional as everyone else in the room. To me, whenever I put on a shirt and tie, it feels like I can do anything.

But my friends often disagree. When they knock on doors, they like to be more casual. Some prefer sneakers and shorts, some prefer khakis and a button down, some prefer sweatshirts and sweatpants. It's all up to you. You will develop your own style, and this will become your brand, no different than New England Patriots Head Coach Bill Belichick and his sweatshirt.[87]

[86] "Never argue with an idiot. They will only bring... - Goodreads." 2012. 21 Nov. 2015 <http://www.goodreads.com/quotes/445589-never-argue-with-an-idiot-they-will-only-bring-you>
[87] "Cutting off the Sleeves: The History of Bill Belichick and His ..." 2013. 21 Nov. 2015 <http://bleacherreport.com/articles/1668165-cutting-off-the-sleeves-the-history-of-bill-belichick-and-his-hoodie>

What to bring?

-Flyers. You should always have a piece of literature in your hand when you knock on doors. As you're giving the voter your elevator speech, you can hand the voter your flyer. Many candidates differ with me on a strategy for flyers; they often prefer to spend a good deal of money on them, with glossy print, fancy design, etc.... I ran in 2012 without a major fundraising operation, so Myles and I decided that a flyer on simple computer paper would cut it. We drafted up a flyer in *Microsoft Word,* and asked my friends who were adults to print a couple hundred copies each in their offices. This way, all we spent was energy, rather than money; we spent our money on lawn signs (to be covered). There's no wrong answer here. If you have some money to spend on glossy print, or if you have a friend who's good with computers, having a fancier flyer does not hurt at all. But if you're like me and are trying to conserve resources, computer paper will absolutely do.

What goes on your flyer? First and foremost, you need your picture so voters remember who you are after they've spoken to you. They'll be inundated with flyers, and even though they may forget your name, they won't forget your face. You of course need your name, and the office you're running for. You should have the election date, especially if you're running for an office where the vote takes place outside of November. You should have important links, such as your website (we'll cover this), and your Facebook page (this too). You should have your contact information (an email address is sufficient). You should have your slogan at the top. If you've been assigned a ballot position (this happens often in nonpartisan elections), then make sure to put it on there and bold it. And most importantly, you should include highlights of your platform; quick bullet points summarizing how you feel about important issues, and summarizing unique ideas that you have. You can and should have expanded explanations of your platform on your website. But for a flyer that a voter will read quickly, it should be concise points that are easily digestible and articulated clearly.

-Petitions. As mentioned previously, if you're knocking on doors, you're going to want to bring your petitions. A great strategy to use, when you're done gathering your signatures, is to send letters to all those who signed your petitions thanking them for helping out your campaign, and reminding them when Election Day is.

-Business Cards. Business cards are great to have on you, as voters will often ask how to get in touch with you. Additionally, you won't have flyers on you at all times. Countless times, whether I was getting a haircut, eating with my buddies in the diner, or watching my brother's baseball games, I would meet voters who liked what I had to say. Handing them a business card, with a link to your website, your email address, and phone number is a great way to bring them into your campaign. I used Vistaprint for my business cards— super easy to design and cheap to order.[88]

-Water. Leaving home at 9:00 a.m. on a Saturday and coming home at 9:00 p.m. is grueling; do yourself a favor and bring a water bottle (or four) with you.

---

[88] "Vistaprint | Business Cards, Postcards, Invitations & More." 22 Nov. 2015 <http://www.vistaprint.com/>

A couple important notes to remember.

If the resident isn't home, leave your flyer on their door! Do NOT put literature in individual residents' mailboxes. Remember the trick I've learned; punch a hole in the top of the piece of paper, tie a rubber band through it, and use the rubber band as a door hanger. Ellen Nesbitt likes to write a little note on the piece of literature she leaves on the door. Everyone has their own style; I promise you'll develop yours as well.

When knocking on doors, there will be voters who want to speak in depth about certain issues. This is wonderful, but be cognizant that you have a finite amount of time and a finite amount of daylight; thus, you can't spend *too* much time at each house (you'll develop a good feel for this). Easiest way to remedy this? Simply hand the resident a business card, and ask them to contact you to set up a meeting so you can speak more in depth about that issue at another time. Morning meetings were my favorite because it would make my mom happy that I'd end up actually eating breakfast before school.

The first impression is everything. It's common knowledge that books do unfortunately get judged by their covers—all the more reason to do your best to make a great presentation. Have confidence in your voice, make eye contact, and give a firm handshake. It's completely normal to be nervous, however the best remedy for nerves is preparation: know your platform, know current events, and you're going to be fine.

When does door knocking not work?

If you live in a rural area like Saira Blair, where the houses are miles apart, door knocking may not be a wise use of your time. Rather than door knocking, Saira opted for mailers instead (we'll cover this). Saira says that, "In my district we couldn't go door to door because we're more rural...there's 2-3 miles between houses." Saira tells me it's a, "40-min drive to the end of my district...it's hard to go out in the evening and knock out 20 houses."

Lawn Signs

What's a political campaign without some lawn signs? Every November the leaves fall from the trees, the ground hardens from frost, and all of the sudden there are more lawn signs blanketing highway dividers than there are actual cars on the road.

Lawn signs are important for a number of reasons. They help establish name recognition with voters. They help boost awareness about the upcoming election. Their most important function? In my opinion, it's to give you validation as a candidate.

Take Anthony Fasano. Anthony, in addition to having "4 X 8 signs," says his campaign had, "Hundreds of lawn signs, most of which were are private property." And for voters who chose to display these signs, "My campaign would deliver them."

Why is this so important? First, Anthony's campaign put on a clinic when it came to voter relations. If a voter wants to help, make it easy for them to do so, whether it's delivering them lawn signs, literature, etc.... **But this is important because when a voter displays your lawn sign on their property, it's the single strongest showing of support a candidate can receive at the local level.**

Having voters display your signs on their property sends a message to your community about the support your campaign has. And it will be huge PR for your campaign. Neighbors will ask the resident about you, and will get to learn about your campaign from an ally rather than an enemy. And residents who have yet to make up their mind about who they're voting for will be influenced by seeing your signs displayed on their street and in their neighborhood.

Campaigns are about shaping a narrative; by getting signs on lawns all over town, the narrative becomes that your campaign has powerful grassroots support.

How do you begin getting these signs all around town? Like starting to build a campaign team, you start with friends and family. I called up one of my best friends Kelly Yuen, and we set out to blanket Syosset with *Vote for Josh Lafazan* lawn signs. Kelly and I left at 2:30 p.m. on that Sunday afternoon in 2012, and didn't get home until midnight—she still holds it over me to this day. **You see, I keep mentioning the role your closest friends play in your campaign because they are the people you can lean on for help.** In keeping with this theme, where was the first and second place we went? Greg Morley's house and then Justin Cristando's, both mentioned in the Introduction as the people by my side when the election results rolled in.

Be strategic where you put your signs. Your best move is to put signs on the lawns of homes in densely trafficked areas. Think next to a school, a church, a busy intersection, etc.... I was lucky to know many people who lived in houses that fit this description (major thanks to Aunt Debbie & Uncle David, Ann & Dan Rizzo, The Sullo family, and many more). If you see a house that's in a great location, ask them to display your sign!

Hello Sir/Ma'am,

My name is Joshua Lafazan, and I am running for a seat on the Syosset School Board of Education. My campaign believes in transparency and open government, teaching 21st century skills to students to best prepare them for the future, ensuring that every dollar spent is spent carefully, and we stand opposed to egregious administrative salaries like that of our current superintendent.

We are out displaying lawn signs all over town in order to get the word out about our campaign. Would you be so kind to let us display a sign on your lawn?

The majority of houses I asked said yes, and thus became allies of my campaign. Some said they wanted to learn more about me first–this is absolutely fine. Give them a flyer and make sure to follow up with them the next week. And for those houses who said no? Don't sweat it, and move on.

Putting signs on public land is also a good move. Be cognizant though that while signs on private property are at the discretion of the homeowner, signs on public land can be taken down by anyone. **Once again, be strategic.** My campaign allocated a portion of signs for public land, and to make them stand out, we put multiple signs together in a row. A driver on the road is more likely to notice five signs together than one single standalone sign. Additionally, we focused on signs on public land towards the end of our campaign; we focused our main attention on getting these signs on lawns.

I keep stressing the importance of being strategic because these signs go fast; in one day, Kelly and I managed to display over half of our first batch of signs.

Next, remember that drivers should easily be able to read these signs from the road. I made this mistake with my first batch of signs. You know how you take an eye exam at the doctor's office, and you have to read the last line to see which way the letters are facing? That was the equivalent of looking at my signs from a distance. Learn from my mistake, and go with less words and bigger font. Thus, similar to your flyer, your name, the office you're running for, ballot position (if you have one), election date, and your slogan should go on your sign; less is more.

In addition to lawns and public land, putting these signs in stores can be quite advantageous, as all shoppers who walk in will see your name. Where do you start? Well, if you know a community member who owns a local business, you should definitely ask them. And if you're a frequent customer at a store, you should ask them as well. A major thank you to Dana Norman and CardSmart Plainview, Don & Debbie Sisun and Ralph's Italian Ices in Syosset, Dugan's Sandwich Shop in Woodbury, Tenjin Sushi, Celebrity Diner, and so many more stores for your support.

In addition to lawn signs, many candidates like Anthony Fasano also opt for bigger signs and banners. These can be expensive, but if you have the money to spend, go for it. **As you know by now, my campaign always looked to stretch a buck when we could, so we decided to get creative. We took three bed sheets from my house, and had my buddy Dylan Pero spray paint them with "Lafazan for Board of Ed."** We then tied two of these banners to a couple of wooden poles we bought at

Home Depot, and lo and behold, we had two massive campaign signs. A major thank you goes out to Alex Kugelman, Jared Swedler, Michael Starr, and Alex Rosenblatt for standing on the corner of Jericho Turnpike and holding these banners (sorry about the cars that honked at you!). Moreover, a major thank you to Ann & Dan Rizzo for letting us hang the third banner on your fence on Cold Spring Road in Syosset.

Lastly, this applies to those candidates who are running on a slate (if you're seeking an office where the top vote getters, as opposed to a single victor, win the election). As I did when I ran this past May for re-election with Andy Feldman and Seth Hart, rather than putting all three names on one sign, simply order three signs with the same design, but put only one candidate's name on each sign. Too often signs with all three names on it are unclear and unreadable. Rather, by having three of the same sign with the different names of the candidates, they are both easily readable, and will stand out to the voter.

If you're looking to order lawn signs for your campaign, I used Image Graphic for both my election and my re-election, and they were nothing short of spectacular.[89] Huge thank you to Stephen Scher for all of your help over the years—you're the best, my friend.

Direct Mail

Direct mailings are an important tool of your campaign; it helps get your literature into the home of a voter.

---

[89] "Image Graphic - banners, dyes fabric printing, vehicle ..." 2002. 22 Nov. 2015 <http://www.imagegraphic.com/>

For Saira Blair, she decided that she wanted to hand write letters instead. As reported by *The Independent*, "First were the handwritten letters—3,500 of them—on her stationery, giving potential voters the location of their nearest polling station and introducing herself to West Virginians. 'Hello! My name is Saira Blair. I am a fiscal Conservative. I'm Pro Life. I'm Pro Marriage. I'm Pro Family. I'm Pro Business because that's where jobs come from.'"[90]

If you're like me, and are getting hand cramps just thinking about writing 3,500 letters, then you may want to opt for direct mail.

Direct mail can be expensive, so many candidates only send one piece per campaign.

A trick I learned is to use the United States Postal Service *Every Door Direct Mail* program. As described on the USPS website, "Just create your mail pieces however you like, then select postal routes and pay for postage online. Next, bring your mailing to your local Post Office for delivery to every household on your chosen routes."[91] So rather than filling out addresses and putting stamps on every piece of literature you want to send, which would take an eternity, you can select the postal routes in your community, and simply deliver your flyers to the Post Office for them to deliver.

For Justin Chenette, he opts to not utilize direct campaign mailers, and instead uses his campaign's "hidden secret"—letters to the editor. Justin explains that his campaign, "Had a letter to the editor in every newspaper each week, and each letter would target a

---

[90] "Saira Blair: the youngest elected state politician in the US ..." 2014. 22 Nov. 2015 <http://www.independent.co.uk/news/world/americas/saira-blair-the-youngest-elected-state-politician-in-the-us-9909114.html>
[91] "Every Door Direct Mail | USPS - USPS.com." 2011. 22 Nov. 2015 <https://www.usps.com/business/every-door-direct-mail.htm>

different topic...this was free publicity, as advertising is expensive." He explained how his campaign would, "Take a 'Letter to the Editor' and expand it from an individual in the neighborhood and send the letters out as if it was from them...we'd send it to all the voters within their ward...each of the letters are hand addressed, and we'd pick people who were relatively well known." He says that people are, "Inundated with campaign mail...it usually ends up in the trash." I admire Justin for his ability to think outside the box, and this is just one example of his ingenuity.

Email

Every young elected official in this book developed their own style as either a candidate or an elected official, and therefore has a "thing" that they're uniquely known for.

For example, U.S. Congressman Justin Amash's "thing" is Facebook. As *The American Conservative* details, "Amash explains all his votes on Facebook, but is especially detailed when discussing these difficult votes."[92]

My "thing" is email. The beauty of this book is that you can take multiple "things" from each different elected official, and develop your own "thing" to use when campaigning or when elected.

I use email for many reasons, but none more important than this: I ran on a platform of transparency and open government, and email has allowed me to include the community in the functioning of the district like never before. Through email, I'm able to apprise

---

[92] "Target: Justin Amash | The American Conservative." 2014. 22 Nov. 2015 <http://www.theamericanconservative.com/articles/target-justin-amash/>

the community of highlights from a school board meeting, and let the community know when an important vote is coming up. I also use email because it gives me a "bully pulpit" to help advance my ideas.[93] Before I introduce an idea at a board meeting, I introduce the idea to the community in an email, supporting it with evidence, and debunking the possible counterarguments. This way, I'm able to drum up support in the community before the idea gets voted on by my colleagues.

So how does email play a role in your campaign? In many different ways.

First, it's a great tool to bring new people into your campaign. Each time I send a campaign email, I ask my supporters to forward that email to five of their friends. Moreover, I ask my supporters to please send me the names and email addresses of those currently not on my email distribution list. This has allowed me to grow my email list by over 25%, and therefore I'm reaching 25% more people than I was beforehand. Secondly, rather than paying for direct mail, I'm able to get my campaign literature into the inbox of voters for free. Lastly, email is great for receiving feedback. Through sending emails I'm able to receive feedback from community members about my ideas, and adjust my platform accordingly.

How do you build an email list? Like everything else in this book, start with friends in family. When I first started out, I went on Facebook and messaged each one of my friends, asking them for their email addresses, and to send me both the names and

[93] "Did You Know? . TR, The Story of Theodore ... - PBS." 2011. 22 Nov. 2015
<http://www.pbs.org/wgbh/americanexperience/features/general-article/tr-know/>

email addresses of their parents. Very quickly you'll be able to build your list up from a few hundred to a few thousand.

Of course you can use Gmail, Hotmail, Yahoo, or any one of the myriad of email sites on the web. However now that I've amassed quite a large list, I use the site MailChimp when I send mass emails.[94] MailChimp allows me to track what percent of my list is opening my emails, what percentage are clicking on links I provide, and cleans up my list by removing inactive email accounts.

If you're using a regular email service, a trick I was taught is to put your entire list in the "bcc" column, and simply put yourself in the "to" column. Doing this means your recipients don't see the other addresses on your email list, and therefore your opponents can't steal your list and use it for their own campaign.

Website

As mentioned previously, every candidate running in the digital age should have a campaign website.

When I was running, I was able to connect with Connor Kurtz and ask him for advice because I found his website online. If you take a look at Connor's website (http://schoolboard.connorkurtz.org/), it's a perfect example of what you need—a very user friendly and simple site.[95] The major gripe adults have with apps like Snapchat is that they're too difficult to use;

---

[94] "MailChimp: Send Better Email." 2004. 22 Nov. 2015 <http://mailchimp.com/>
[95] "Connor Kurtz - School Director for Amity Township." 2011. 23 Nov. 2015 <http://schoolboard.connorkurtz.org/>

your site should be easily navigable by *anybody* with a computer.[96]

Connor's site has four simple tabs: Home, Issues, About Connor, and Contact Connor. This is all you need on your website. When people come to your site they should be able to learn about you, so put your biography on there. They should be able to learn about what you stand for, so put your platform with explanations for each issue on there. And they should be able to contact you, so put a contact form on there.

If you have a friend who's good with computers, or have some money to spend on a web designer, then your site can look a little sleeker, like Nicole Malliotakis' (http://nicolemalliotakis.com/), where she features a weekly poll that her constituents can take part in.[97]

I'm lucky that my little brother Aaron Lafazan is a computer whiz—he designed my website, and I recommend him for any young candidate who's looking to make a campaign website.[98]

Something I use for my site, as does Nicole and many others, is an option for people who visit my site to join my email list. If you go to my website (http://www.joshlafazan.com/), before you enter it gives the viewer an opportunity to join my mailing list.[99] This has been a huge tool to grow my list, and another example of how concepts in this book build off each other.

---

[96] "The adult's guide to Snapchat." 2015. 23 Nov. 2015 <http://www.businessesgrow.com/2015/06/10/guide-to-snapchat/>
[97] "Nicole Malliotakis for New York State Assembly." 2010. 23 Nov. 2015 <http://nicolemalliotakis.com/>
[98] "Aaron Lafazan." 2015. 23 Nov. 2015 <https://www.AaronLafazan.com>
[99] "Joshua Lafazan." 2013. 23 Nov. 2015 <http://www.joshlafazan.com/>

Squarespace is a new and easy to use tool to make a website, which requires very minimal knowledge of computers. It's $8.00 a month to make a web page.[100]

Phone Banking, Robocalls & Textathons

No matter the political movie you are watching, there is always a scene where volunteers are making phone calls at the campaign's headquarters. The ubiquitousness of this scene isn't an accident; **phone calls are an important part of each and every campaign.**

Almost all of your volunteers will have cell phones, thus you'll only need to supply them with a call sheet. You can give them a list of numbers you get from the Board of Elections, community directories, or a host of other places. Just be conscious to remind them that all calls should be made before 8:00 p.m. or so, as you want to be respectful of people in your community such as senior citizens and parents with young children. Some campaigns provide volunteers with two scripts: one for if they reach a voter over the phone, and one if they get a voter's voicemail. When my volunteers get a voter on the phone, I like to give them the autonomy to talk to the voter—I trust my volunteers to have my back. I simply ask my volunteers to remind the voters of when Election Day is, and to inquire if the voter knows where his/her polling location is. However, when my volunteers reach a voter's voicemail, I give them the following script:

---

[100] "Squarespace: Build a Website." 2003. 29 Nov. 2015 <http://www.squarespace.com/>

Good evening!

My name is Jon Iavarone, and I'm a campaign volunteer at Joshua Lafazan for Syosset School Board.

I'm calling to remind you that Election Day is in two weeks, on Tuesday, May 15th, from 6:00 a.m. until 10:00 p.m. Voters cast their votes at their local elementary school.

If you need a ride to the polls on Election Day, would like a lawn sign, or more information on Joshua Lafazan and his ideas for the Syosset School District, please call us at (516)-123-4567 and we'd be happy to help.

Thank you for your time, and remember to vote for Joshua Lafazan on Ballot Position #5 so that Syosset can thrive!

Very simple, very short, with all necessary information, as well as an option for the voter to get more information. Feel free to copy this script, or to change it completely; you just need to shoot for consistency.

Robocalls are another tool to utilize during your campaign. For this option you'll need two things: a phone list and a recording. You can purchase a list of phone numbers online, but make sure that these numbers are for voters in your voting district; the last thing you want to do is spend money on a list of voters for a neighboring town where people can't vote for you. For a recording, all you need is a smart phone. For my re-election, I did my recording, as well as those for my running mates, in the Voice Memos app on my iPhone. For the robocalls I used a service called Robodial, which

I found pretty easy to use.[101] With Robodial, I simply uploaded my list of phone numbers, uploaded my recording, set a time for the phone call, and lo and behold, thousands of voters would receive a call with my voice. What's cool about using Robodial is that it sends you a detailed report of how many calls went to voicemail, how long into the call people listened, etc.... A strategy I used was to vary the theme of these recordings: my first recording introduced my running mates and me, the second recording gave voters information about our platform, and the last recording was a reminder to come out and vote. Prices vary by the length of the recording, but 30 seconds is your cheapest option.

Lastly, textathons are a new Millennial phenomenon. **You're young—this book implores you to use your youth to your advantage, rather than running away from it!** Thus something my campaign did, and something I definitely recommend for your campaign, is to host a textathon.

Yes, kids are on social media. But, generally speaking, all kids text; it's the dominant form of communication among Millennials. I know this because whenever I ask my best friend at Cornell, Nicole Battipaglia, to hang out she reminds me that if I want to make plans with her I should text her and not send her a iPhone calendar invite (she declines these).

So the week before my election, I gathered a ton of friends in a room, bought a bunch of pizzas, put on some music, and held a textathon, where each kid would text every Syosset resident in their phone's contact list to come out and vote. **We reached over**

---

[101] "Squarespace: Build a Website." 2003. 29 Nov. 2015 <http://www.squarespace.com/>

2,000 unique voters, and the majority were ages 18-29, a demographic that does not vote.[102] By having everyone together, it actually turned into a fun event. And all it costs you is a couple pizza pies and a tip for the delivery guy.

Social Media

Social media use has forever changed the political landscape. As Tom Murse writes, social media has, "Made politicians more accountable and accessible at the same time allowing campaigns to carefully craft and customize their candidates' images based on rich sets of analytics in real time and at almost no cost."[103]

The use of social media as a campaign tool is something the young elected officials in this book used proficiently. Take Chase Harrison.

Chase says that:

> "My main campaign tool was my Facebook page. I loved using the page because I was able to reach students and parents alike and it gave me demographic breakdowns of who was viewing the page. It also allowed for responsiveness. If I posted a campaign stance, someone could respond with their suggestions. Comments and likes allowed me to gauge which issues sparked

---

[102] "Millennials don't believe in voting - The Boston Globe." 2015. 23 Nov. 2015 <https://www.bostonglobe.com/opinion/2015/08/20/millennials-don-believe-voting/cGb7sx5ZvkmDCsNd3shTDO/story.html>

[103] "How Social Media Has Changed Politics - US Politics." 2013. 23 Nov. 2015 <http://uspolitics.about.com/od/CampaignsElections/tp/How-Social-Media-Has-Changed-Politics.htm>

the largest reaction from my supporters. I was also able to post videos from debates, news articles, and invites to campaign events. It was really the interactivity that made it a better tool than a traditional website."

Additionally, take Chris Scales. Chris said his, "Most effective campaign material was free, social media. I launched a Facebook page and posted my platform along with articles covering the school board race. In just a few weeks, more than 300 people were following my campaign. With the help of local unions, they were going door-to-door on behalf of me as well."

However, social media can also be a negative. As Chase warns, **"Cleanse and lock up all social media accounts. If someone is looking for dirt on you, they will find innocent things and project them as examples of your immaturity."**

There are many different social media outlets. You can use one or all of them, it doesn't matter; this campaign is yours—don't be afraid to experiment.

For my campaign, I put Jake Asman and Dan Budick in charge of social media. They had an excellent track record of getting hundreds of views on each video posted of their sports radio show, and their help solidified a key principle I live by; **don't be afraid to surround yourself with those who know more about a certain subject then you. This is the only way you can truly learn.**

Jake says that, "Social media played a huge role in the campaign because we wanted to be able to reach out to the younger generation and encourage them to get involved in local politics. We felt that we had to expose Josh's platform to as many people as possible, and through social media we were able to share Josh's ideas and campaign announcements with the community instantly."

And Dan agrees that, "Social media played a huge part in the campaign because it sent Josh's message to people who otherwise wouldn't know what he stood for and what he was saying. Both Jake and I felt that by using social media it would enhance his campaign and allow him to express his views in new ways."

We found Facebook to be the best tool to connect with every demographic (excluding senior citizens). And we found Twitter to be the best tool to connect with celebrities, reporters and pundits; even ESPN Football Analyst Adam Schefter tweeted us his best wishes![104]

But our most effective tool during my first election? Hosting virtual town halls on Spreecast.[105] As the digital media giant *Mashable* reported, "On Spreecast, Lafazan engaged in face-to-face town halls with his soon-to-be constituency."[106] With Jake and Dan moderating, voters were able to ask me questions directly online via a video feed, and our virtual town hall had over 25,000 views. We were one of the first campaigns nationally to adopt this strategy, and it goes hand-in-hand with my platform; what's more transparent than getting to ask the candidate questions directly in real time?

---

[104] "Timeout from NFL to wish Joshua Lafazan, the first 18-year ..." 2012. 23 Nov. 2015 <http://www.broncosforums.com/forums/showthread.php/266728-AdamSchefter-Timeout-from-NFL-to-wish-Joshua-Lafazan-the-first-18-year-old-to-run-for-the-Syosset-School-Board-of-Education-the-best-in-his-election>

[105] "Spreecast." 2011. 23 Nov. 2015 <http://www.spreecast.com/>

[106] "HS Student's Social-Media-Fueled Campaign ... - Mashable." 23 Nov. 2015 <http://mashable.com/2012/05/21/josh-lafazan-social-media/>

Videos

Campaign videos were a huge asset to my campaign, and I have my buddy Zach Hammer to thank for this. Zach, a student at Brown University, was my classmate at Syosset High school, and an incredibly talented filmmaker. We brought him on board to run our digital media strategy, and it paid major dividends. Zach's first idea was to film a video introducing me to the community, and announcing my run for the school board. The video was set with me driving around town in my car, talking about how I spent my entire life in Syosset, and why I was so passionate to help make it an even better place to live and raise a family. This video received thousands of views, and helped generate buzz about my candidacy throughout the community. Our next video however was our biggest hit—a fun and upbeat video following my campaign volunteers as they put up flyers across Syosset (if you want to see how the rubber band technique works, check out this video).[107] Zach also had me film short 1-2 minute videos, explaining the major points of my platform in detail. These were also a hit, and remain on my website to this day.[108]

If you have a friend who knows how to make videos, that's your best bet. But now with computers, videos can be made with your smart phone. Whatever way you choose to make them, make sure to put them up on social media and have your friends share them. **We live in the digital age; a single video can**

---

[107] "OCT: Flyers on Vimeo." 2015. 26 Nov. 2015
<https://vimeo.com/38753793>
[108] "Future Initiatives - Joshua Lafazan." 2013. 26 Nov. 2015
<http://www.joshlafazan.com/future-initiatives.html>

reach thousands of people in no time without costing you a dime.

Fundraising

Ah, we finally have come to fundraising.

Former Congressman Romano Mazzoli once said that, "People who contribute get the ear of the member and the ear of the staff. They have the access and access is it. Access is power. Access is clout. That's how this thing works."[109]

Unfortunately, he's not wrong. In fact, a study from Princeton suggests that America is no longer a democracy, but rather an oligarchy ruled by wealthy elites.[110]

So when people ask me how Millennials are going to change politics, this is precisely what I'm talking about—we will work for *all* of the people. We will work for those who contribute to candidates, and those who don't, and *everybody* will have our ear. Because this is the conduct we expect from our representatives. And it's specifically this disappointment in our representatives today that fuels our desire to lead the *right* way—where we prioritize no one, and fight for everyone.

Remember what Saira Blair said earlier: **"I wanted to make sure people knew I would fight for every resident, and not just the connected."**

---

[109] "Campaign Finance Quotes - Public Citizen Access to Justice ..." 2010. 26 Nov. 2015
<http://www.citizen.org/congress/article_redirect.cfm?ID=5723>
[110] "Princeton Study: U.S. No Longer An Actual Democracy." 2014. 26 Nov. 2015 <http://talkingpointsmemo.com/livewire/princeton-experts-say-us-no-longer-democracy>

Fundraising does however play a crucial role in any election, without a doubt. For my campaign, I chose not to solicit donations or establish a large scale fundraising effort. I am so grateful that, unsolicited, I received donations from people across my community; their support is humbling beyond words. But I chose to focus my efforts at the grassroots level, spending money on lawn signs and a direct mailer, and focusing my time knocking on doors, reaching out to Millennial voters, and ensuring that every kid in school dragged their parents down to the polls on Election Day. **You have to gauge your own race.** If you're running for your local school board of Education like I did, and have the ability to knock on every door and meet people at the local level, then maybe you won't need to raise a ton of cash. But if you're running for a larger position, like a seat in Congress, you're going to have to fundraise.

So this chapter will focus on those elected officials who were quite successful fundraising. First, we'll start with Michaelle Solages.

Michaelle Solages does not understate the difficulty of fundraising for a political race. She says that, "One of the most challenging aspects of running for office is asking for money...it can make or break a candidate." Michaelle advises young candidates to not be narrow in your focus when raising money—"I think you should ask anyone and everyone for a contribution. You have to raise money. It's a necessary evil." She also says that you, **"Can't be shy about it, you have to get on the phone and ask people to invest in your cause and vision."**

Michaelle also feels it's extra difficult to raise money as a woman. She says that it's, "Always hard for women to raise money, because we don't like to ask for things, we just do it." (She laughs as she tells me to think about my mom as an example of a woman who doesn't ask, but rather just does.) Michaelle is an example of why you should not discount the importance of small contributions to help propel you to victory. She implores young candidates to not, "Be shy about getting any amount of money." She continues, **"$10, $5, $3 dollars" will be valuable to your campaign.** How? "If you call someone for $100, and only get $5, it's still important because it can be used to buy water or food for your door knocker...use it wisely."

Saira Blair is in agreement with Michaelle about the difficulty of fundraising. She feels that, "Fundraising is definitely the hardest part," of your campaign, and she says that this isn't associated with age, but rather, "It's just something you have to be comfortable with." For Saira, it's something she says she still struggles with to this day (Saira laughs as she tells me this, because she says she should be starting to raise money now for her re-election). Saira, "Raised about $30,000" for her race, which is quite an impressive haul for any candidate, let alone a teenager. **Saira tells me she, "Sent in $4,000 of my own money" (which was a loan to herself as this was money for her first semester of college). She did this to, "Put some skin in the game,"** which signaled to all of her donors that she was serious about the race, and would spend her contributions wisely.

How did she fundraise? Similar to everything in this book—she started with those closest to her! She, "Reached out to parents, brothers, aunts, uncles, asked family friends," and advises young candidates to, "Keep reaching out and going around different circles you have starting from the center." So yes, start with mom and dad, and work your way out to the extended family. But you can definitely ask your friends' parents, friends of the family, and those people you touch from all the different organizations you're a part of. **Being a**

Millennial, use social media and the internet to your advantage as well! Saira says that, "Once I hit a wall, we set up online donations, and reached out on social media" to get contributions from Facebook friends and website visitors. The results? She, "Received about 20% of donations from people that I didn't know."

For Das Williams, he feels that hopping on the phone is the most crucial thing a candidate can do to raise money. He says that, **"The most important part of fundraising is being willing to make the calls.** I made calls for hours on end to friends, supporters from my city council days, family members, and other potential donors." Das is another example of how concepts in this book build upon each other. Remember that Das worked on his first political campaign at age 17, and worked on a myriad of others in his twenties. He says that, "Luckily I had worked as an organizer on campaigns throughout the state so I had many connections and wasn't afraid to use those connections, do the work, and make the calls." **Das also stresses how fundraising is not about *you*, but about your community as a whole**. "I feel like something that makes fundraising intimidating for some candidates is feeling like you're asking for a personal favor." He continues, "I ran for the assembly to work for my community and asking people for donations was a way to invite them to be a part of the team. It was never about me as an individual, it was about what we could do together for the community."

In 2015, $600 likely isn't sufficient to purchase college books for one semester. Marcus Molinaro ran for a village trustee seat in Tivoli in 1994 (the same year I was born). That year, his entire campaign cost $600. Marcus says that, "Raising money wasn't a priority because I went to every house three times." He brings up an important point here; **money does not guarantee a winner, and the lack of it doesn't guarantee a loser.** There are things money can buy, and there are things money cannot—truly being a "man of the people" like Marcus is, and speaking to residents while knocking on every door three times in your community is something that you just can't buy.

Marcus says that, "I don't dislike fundraising, I despise fundraising...I despise the whole process (he laughs as he articulates his distaste for political fundraising). He says there are, "Two things you have to appreciate." First, **"Most candidates don't know what they need to spend in order to win, so they end up spending more money than what they need."** He equates this to the law of diminishing returns. So in this realm, make a budget before you run for office including how expensive things are, and what your target fundraising level is. This will alter how aggressive you have to be as a fundraiser, and as Marcus suggests, will actually save you money in the long run. An example he provides is the late, "Flurry of mail and phone calls and television ads that people block out and don't mean anything," Secondly, he says that, **"Consultants want more money."** He jokes that candidates, "Hire consultants to tell us to spend more money." So he believes that, "These two things create a bloated system."

Marcus agrees that there's, "Little question that New York State is a corrupt democratic process." So from his experience in village government, he feels there's a sharp difference in efficacy between money and personability. He feels that, **"The most effective way to earn a vote is to actually earn it by showing up**... [contributions] are an unfortunate part of the process that would be nice if it changed." I make it no secret that I have deep respect and admiration for the Dutchess County Executive, and here's why–he's one of the most honest elected officials I've ever met. He says that, "I get into trouble because I disclose things that are allowed...I readily admit that I was a poor guy when I came into this office, living at home with two kids, so I went out and bought some clothes...to look like an executive." So does he take grief for this? Yes. But can anyone ever fault him for his lack of honesty or transparency? Absolutely not. I wish we had more of this type of attitude from representatives nationwide.

If anybody in this book knows how to fundraise, it's Ian Calderon–he raised $936,693 for his re-election campaign in 2014, and $792,555 during the cycle before.[111] Ian says that, "I was very fortunate to have my father...because of his long career, I could use his relationships to help me with fundraising." But it was Ian who put in the work and made the fundraising happen, not his dad. Ian tells me that, "Dad is not giving me all my money, I *personally* made hundreds and thousands of calls to try to raise money, sat down with people personally...my father definitely helped, but people always overlooked that I had to give the pitch, I had to convince these people I was going to win and why I was going to win."

Like Marcus Molinaro, Ian also has a distaste for fundraising, sharing with me that, "I hate fundraising...to have to sit down, call someone who you don't know at all and ask for money is one of the hardest things to do." Moreover, Ian notes the sharp contrast between fundraising for a political endeavor versus a philanthropic one, when you say that you're

---

[111] "Ian Charles Calderon - Ballotpedia." 2015. 26 Nov. 2015
<https://ballotpedia.org/Ian_Charles_Calderon>

calling, "Not to help a great cause or charity, but it's asking for money to help me win...it's a very nerve wracking thing." As earlier, when I mentioned how those who achieve success are the ones who ask for help, in the same vein, those who take advantage of the help available to them achieve success as well. Look no further than Ian—"I took advantage of all the help that I could get...a combination of my father's relationships and me making phone calls and doing the meetings...I wanted to be an individual, and even though they knew me because of my father, I could prove to them that standing alone as an individual...I could stand on my own two feet, make tough and right choices and properly represent my district."

Lastly, Ian feels that the importance of fundraising was the ability to get his message out to the public. He says, **"If I can't send people mail to tell them who I am, what I campaigned and delivered on, what I want to do...I can't be here, I can't win, I can't be elected...the only way to do it is to raise money."**

Cyrus Habib tells me that, "I've been very lucky in my fundraising to come into this with a really healthy network of supporters." However Cyrus, unlike most candidates, represents an area with some of the country's most prominent innovators. He jokes that, "It doesn't hurt that my district which I represent is very well off...I have Bill Gates and Jeff Bezos [Amazon CEO] as constituents." He continues saying, "It definitely helps because a lot of people here made money in technology, and they're inclined to support Democrats...a lot of them became really successful at a young age." Cyrus also says he had, "Good support from fellow alumni, and the Iranian American community."

Like every elected official interviewed, Cyrus recognizes the challenges of raising money—"For younger candidates who don't have a professional network, it can be difficult to raise money." **But he cautions all young candidates to stop, and, "Think about what the money is there for."** Cyrus says it's there for "voter contact," such as: "A field program, sending direct mail, or television ads if it's a big enough race." As I mentioned before, there are things money can buy, and things it cannot; something it cannot buy you is motivated supporters. Cyrus feels that, "Someone who's 22, 23 that has a large network of energetic young people who have the energy and vigor and desire to do a lot of volunteer field work," can be a game changer in a race. He continues that an army of volunteers can definitely be more powerful than having money in the bank. And because you're young, Cyrus says you, "Have easier access to field support...having an army of fifteen college classmates, friends...a young person who knows you personally, can talk about you...I would take that over getting money for stamps to send mailers to people who will probably throw it away anyway. It's not about the money, it's about what the money can buy." In this same realm, **"If you can post a big number [of contributions] and scare someone from the race, that's good...but it's just as intimidating if you have a video on your website of 150 kids who are starting to knock on doors."**

For Justin Chenette, he says that he was, "Fundraising on my own when I first ran," as he was in a contested primary for the Democratic nomination. What role did fundraising play for Justin? He recalls how his, "Opponent tried to capitalize on my being young, having no 'real world experience,' so I had to outspend the opponent to anticipate negativity."

Nicole Malliotakis is the epitome of how things in this world come full circle. When asked about fundraising, Nicole says that, "I had no support from unions in 2010, now I'm the ranking member of the committee [on Government Employees]."[112] Nicole also now enjoys wide support from organizations such as the AFL-CIO and the FDNY.[113] Nicole feels that, **"People don't want to go against the incumbent."** So instead her first campaign, "Was grassroots," raising money, "From individuals who were very affected and concerned." Nicole says she was, "Outspent 2.5-1." She jokes that, "We still won." How did she do it? She was passionate about her message for a better working government, a more accountable government, and a government that worked once again for the people. And she took this message to every corner of her district–something I urge every young candidate to do in their races,

    If you're reading this and have yet to raise any money, please do not think for a second that you cannot win. Ellen Nesbitt says that she, "Didn't hold any fundraisers...we spent around $2,000 max, that was our own money." She instead says that she ran, "A very grassroots campaign...just went door-to-door," noting the help of her dad, mom, sister, and brothers.

    It's important to remember two things.

    First, be cognizant of the rules of fundraising for your campaign. These rules should be readily available to you when you file your petitions or can be found on the website of your local municipality. Most likely you're going to need to set up

---

[112] "New York State Assembly | Nicole Malliotakis." 2015. 26 Nov. 2015 <http://assembly.state.ny.us/mem/Nicole-Malliotakis/story/63156/>

[113] "FDNY unions back Staten Island's Malliotakis, saying she ..." 2012. 26 Nov. 2015 <http://sigop.com/fdny-unions-back-staten-islands-malliotakis-saying-she-fought-fire-company-closings/

a new bank account for your campaign, as you SHOULD NOT deposit any of the money you raise into your personal account. You may also need to designate someone as the treasurer of your campaign.

Secondly, stay organized! Keep track of who donates to your campaign, and the amount of their donation. You're going to have to report your donations repeatedly during your campaign.

Candidate Debate

Almost every race you participate in will have some sort of organized debate that is open to the public.

Chase Harrison says that, "My biggest campaign tool was the two debates. I was a very competitive debater in high school, so this was very much my territory. I was able to show my knowledge on all issues, and call my opponent's policies into question."

If you're a competitive debater like Chase, or a great public speaker, you will excel in these debates. If you're not, I promise you'll still do great, as long as you prepare. Heed the sage words of Thomas Jefferson: **"I am a great believer in luck, and I find the harder I work, the more I have of it."**[114]

The way you prepare is to read up on current events relative to the race you're running for! If you're running for a seat in the county legislature, you should know backwards and forwards the issues facing the county, about its budget, about its workforce, about its parks and buildings, and so on. Running for the Syosset School Board, I read *Education Weekly*, I read op-eds

---

[114] "I Am a Great Believer in Luck, and I Find the Harder I Work ..." 2015. 26 Nov. 2015 <http://www.theseeds4life.com/i-am-a-great-believer-in-luck-and-i-find-the-harder-i-work-the-more-i-have-of-it-thomas-jefferson>

and editorials and news stories, I read the superintendent's contract, and other pertinent information relating to public education and the Syosset School District. And to this day I read *On Board,* a publication for school board members. **You will never be faulted for being too well read, and knowing too much; you almost definitely will be faulted however for knowing too little.**

Handling Adversity

As Americans, we love a number of things. We love the free samples in the aisles at Costco. We love cheese in a can. We love Beyoncé. And we most certainly love political drama. If you're lucky enough to avoid any adversity in your race, congratulations; you've avoided a ton of stress, a bunch of headaches, and probably an ulcer. But if I'm a betting man, I'm putting money on your having at least some adversity during your race. Therefore, that "stomach of steel" we keep talking about? This is the time to use it. When adversity strikes, we get a true glimpse into what's inside us. **When the going gets tough, the tough get going.** If I hadn't developed a "stomach of steel" all throughout my campaign, I wouldn't have been prepared to handle what happened the afternoon before my election, when disaster struck—something that will forever live in infamy in Syosset's history, known colloquially to all as *The Robocall.*

The event was so complicated, so outrageous, and so unbelievable, so rather than telling the story myself, I am simply going to give you the way it was reported in its entirety by *The Syosset-Jericho Tribune,* with the following headline:

Residents Irate After Syosset CSD Uses School Emergency Information Network In Alleged Smear Campaign:

Newcomers DiFilippo, Lafazan elected to the school board in the wake of robocalling scandal

"After an eventful and often contentious spring campaign, newcomers Chris DiFilippo and 18-year-old SHS senior class president Josh Lafazan were elected to the Syosset School Board, while incumbent Alan Resnick was re-elected. The arrival of some new faces on the board is newsworthy here, especially since both of the newly-elected trustees have been critical of many district policies. However, a bizarre event the day before the May 15 election threatened to overshadow the results: an accusation of theft levied by the district at Lafazan's father, Jeffrey Lafazan, the use of the school's emergency information network to broadcast that accusation, and the counter-accusation by the Lafazan family that the entire thing was a fabricated crime designed in an attempt to discredit Lafazan's candidacy with a last-minute smear campaign.

After Lafazan's landslide victory on Tuesday, May 15, residents are left with an interesting question: Did Lafazan capture so many more votes than his fellow candidates despite the fact that the district allegedly tried to connect him with a crime, or perhaps because of it? For many residents who may have been ambivalent about the district, the use of the school's emergency network in this manner appeared to push them past their breaking point, so much so that they took their revenge on the status quo at the polls on Tuesday.

The Situation: We Are Not Making This Up

Syosset School District posted a notice on its website on Monday, May 14, that Jeffrey Lafazan removed district election original records (names and addresses of those who applied for absentee ballots). According to the notice, Lafazan removed the records without permission and ran away, and a chase with security ensued. However, according to Lafazan, he was manipulated to take the records out of the building, with no knowledge that they were the originals, so that the district could allege that he knowingly stole them.

Lafazan told Anton Newspapers Monday evening, May 14, that he was initially refused access to the records in the morning, then the school district called him on his cell phone with the news that he would be allowed to see the records after he complained to the New York State Board of Elections. Returning to the school midday, he said he was given the absentee ballot records by a clerk, Christine Costa, who then walked out of the room, at which point he walked to his car; he went on to say that security footage, if available, will confirm that no chase took place. When Lafazan became aware that the district had accused him online of stealing the records, and in automated calls to residents, his wife tried to return said records, only to find the school on lockdown due to a bomb threat, Lafazan said.

A representative from the district's public relations firm, Zimmerman-Edelson said that there was no bomb threat in the district that day, only in neighboring district Jericho. The representative did not offer an explanation for why Mrs. Lafazan was not allowed into the school to return the records if there was no bomb threat. Beyond that communication, the district refused to talk to the Syosset-Jericho Tribune about this event.

Lafazan believes that this alleged theft, which led to robocalls throughout the district to inform residents that Lafazan had "stolen" the papers, was a last-ditch attempt by a desperate administration to smear Lafazan's son's name in the community on the eve of the election.

After the incident had received a fair amount of media coverage, with most outlets seemingly favoring Lafazan's side of the story, the school district released the following statement in defense of its actions on Tuesday, May 15:

"Syosset Central School District sent an autodial message to the community in an effort to recover stolen district records which included confidential information and names and addresses of residents who had submitted applications for absentee ballots. The autodial message asked the Syosset community for help in recovering the missing absentee ballot documents and specifically asked for anyone with information regarding the theft and any individuals involved in the theft to aid the district's search by contacting the Nassau County Police Department."

However, was the information that Jeffrey Lafazan requested really confidential? And if so, whose fault was it that he walked out with it?

Joshua A. Lafazan

FOILed Again: District Caught In A Lie

It turns out that the answer is a little complicated, but not impossible to ascertain. According to the Freedom of Information Law (FOIL), documents from an agency may be withheld when disclosure would result in "an unwarranted invasion of personal privacy" (FOIL Section 87, 2-b.) One situation considered an invasion of privacy is if the "sale or release of lists of names and addresses if such lists would be used for solicitation or fund-raising purposes" (FOIL Section 89, 2b iii).

It seems unlikely that a list of absentee voters names and addresses would be used in this manner the day before an election, but the section of FOIL that deals with invasions of privacy is somewhat nebulous: some would consider the fact that addresses appear on the document at all as reason enough to withhold it under the privacy exception.

However, it was not up to Lafazan to determine whether or not it was appropriate for him to ask for the documents; FOIL encourages citizens to ask for documents from governing bodies. It was up to the district to determine whether or not they considered the request a potential invasion of privacy, and to act accordingly.

If the district believed that giving out the names and addresses of absentee ballot voters constituted an invasion of privacy, they could have told Lafazan that they were denying him access under the relevant FOIL clause (which he could have then challenged, but that's another story). Neither Lafazan nor the district claim that FOIL was cited as the reason why the district initially refused to let him see the document, meaning the district either didn't know about the privacy clause, or didn't think it would hold up as a valid reason to withhold the document under legal scrutiny.

They also had yet another option—FOIL allows agencies to give out censored versions of documents in cases where invasion of privacy is a concern: "The committee on open government may promulgate guidelines regarding deletion of identifying details or withholding of records otherwise available under this article to prevent unwarranted invasions of personal privacy. In the absence of such guidelines, an agency may delete identifying details when it makes records available," (FOIL Section 89 2A).

So if the district was concerned about voter privacy, they legally had the option to give Lafazan a version of the document with some of the information blacked out; they choose not to do so.

While FOIL is complex, after taking all of the above clauses into account it appears that the statement the district issued on May 15 cannot be strictly true. If the district considered the information "confidential," they had the choice to either refuse its release, or censor it accordingly. Instead, they showed the document in question to Lafazan (meaning they did not consider the information contained therein an invasion of privacy), then claimed that the information constituted an invasion of privacy after they had already given it to him. There is nothing in the law that says this determination can be made retroactively.

Even if the district's allegation that Lafazan took the document and ran is true, which Lafazan characterizes as "ridiculous," the district would still be responsible for showing Lafazan information that they had deemed an exception to FOIL due to privacy concerns.

There is also the issue of whether or not the documents Lafazan was given were the originals; Typically, documents requested under FOIL are photocopied, with the individual who makes the request paying for the cost of the copy. If the district chose to give him the only copy of the absentee voters' information, even temporarily, it is neither clear why they would do so, nor why they would assume Lafazan knew he had the original document.

Of course, one could just ignore the finer points of open government laws and just go with Jeffrey Lafazan's reason why the district's official statement doesn't hold water: "If they wanted the documents back, why didn't they just call me on my cell phone? Like they had a half an hour before?"

Residents Sound Off On 'Syossetgate'

Many residents were confused and worried when they received calls from the district in the middle of the day.

"At 2:30 p.m., while my child was in school, I saw that the incoming call was coming from the school and my stomach lurched. Was she sick? Hurt? Was it the principal? Teacher?" recounted Frances Ajamian Ktenas, whose daughter attends Berry Hill Elementary School.

"This was an egregious misuse of the emergency call system. As I understand it the system is supposed to be used for early dismissals, snow days, and other school/student related emergencies," said Ktenas, going on to say that she and many of her fellow parents were outraged by this choice on the part of the district. Ktenas told the Syosset-Jericho Tribune that she tried to find out from the superintendent's office who had authorized the robocall, but received no answer even after getting through to a district employee. The Syosset-Jericho Tribune is continuing to investigate who authorized the robocall.

Fellow resident Charles Nicholas, an attorney, had a similar experience. "When I got the call, the first thing I thought was that it was an emergency...then when you hear that message, what goes through your mind is 'what possessed someone to authorize using this system for this, which is used for the children's safety?" posed Nicholas.

"Then I thought, this is very sad. These are educators who we look toward to safeguard our children," said Nicholas, going on to say that the use of the emergency system for political gain was unfair and a flagrant abuse of power. Nicholas also noted that the abuse of power reminded him of Watergate, leading him to dub the pre-election scandal "Syossetgate."

Other residents were disappointed in how the district had conducted itself over the past few months in general, before Syossetgate.

"Our purpose as parents is to teach our children the importance of participating in the governing establishment, whether local, state, or national. To stand up and challenge the status quo when they see fit. The mudslinging that went on was unacceptable. I received a few "confidential" emails asking me to vote for candidates and the tactics used to gain my vote completely turned me off to those candidates," said Amy Ciotta, financial analyst. "On another note, the grave misuse of the school emergency information network needs to be investigated."

Whether or not Syosset's use of its automatic calling system comes under even more scrutiny, one thing is for sure: if this entire situation was an attempt at a smear campaign against Lafazan on the part of the district, as he and his supporters believe, it seems to have backfired spectacularly. While many parents contacted the Syosset-Jericho Tribune after Monday's robocalls (not all of whom wished to be quoted), not a single one said they believed that the district's accusation of theft was legitimate.

"Why would you smear this kid? Why would you do this to his career? All for what—because he participated in the democratic process?" asked Nicholas, rhetorically. Why, indeed."[115]

---

[115] "Residents Irate After Syosset CSD Uses School Emergency ..." 2012. 26 Nov. 2015
<http://www.antonnews.com/syossetjerichotribune/news/22956-residents-irate-after-syosset-csd-uses-school-emergency-information-network-in-alleged-smear-campaign.html>

If your first reaction is that of complete shock, imagine how I felt, the day before the biggest day of my life as this all transpired.

How did I receive wind of *The Robocall?* Well first, I got a call from News Channel 12 during math class, asking if they could come to my house after school and interview my dad and me. While this sounded great, I was a definitely curious as to why they wanted to interview my dad. Then, things got really weird. My phone was buzzing like crazy with calls from *everyone.* My buddy Cliff Heller (who got up at 6:00 a.m. to go vote before school) called me and told me emphatically, "Dude, whatever they're saying about your dad, this whole town knows it's bullsh*t." While this was quite sweet, I didn't know at that point what was being said about my dad! Then my friend from kindergarten, Alex Oshinsky, texted me, "Bro is everything alright with you and your family? Always here for you." I was getting worried at this point. Things became very real for me, however, when I received a call from my little brother Aaron, eleven years old at the time, crying and asking me if, "Dad is going to jail."

When adversity strikes, in that moment, you have to be the calmest, and the most focused. If we would have panicked, or thrown our hands in the air and given up, I wouldn't be here writing this book right now. But instead, we gathered our composure, took a collective deep breath, and only then, did we take action. Sitting in what my family now jokingly calls "the war room" (my kitchen counter), my brother Justin, my dad, and I went to work. I got on the phone, and called every single assignment desk for every major television news station. It was imperative for us to get our side of the story out quickly, to help stem the tide of fear and misinformation. My brother Justin then coordinated interview times with the television stations and gave directions to news truck drivers. And my dad, in between fielding calls from television stations, crafted our message to be blasted out on social media. By day's end, my dad and I must have given at least a dozen interviews in what we now call "the green room" (the den in my house). Looking back, there were so many takeaways from that day. **First, nobody will listen to somebody who simply complains.** If we would have went on television and just complained about the situation, it would have appeared that we were just whining. But rather, when interviewed, we had a logical, concise, and consistent message–this list was open to the public, and the robocall was a last-minute and desperate attempt by the district to reverse the momentum my campaign had built.

Secondly, the press is a powerful tool. Without the press, the real story–the *truth*–would have never gotten out to the public, and I very well could have lost that election. I'm thankful each and every day for those reporters who came to my house to hear directly from my dad and me and subsequently helped the community gather all the facts before they went to the ballot box.

Thirdly, never underestimate the ability of social media. Through Facebook and Twitter, we were given a platform to share our side of the story. And it quickly spread like wildfire. As reported by *Mashable*, "When the school district tried to pull their smear campaign, Josh hopped on Facebook and sent out a status with what had really happened...It got 250 likes and 200 shares. People very quickly realized what was happening."[116] I share my story, this account of *The*

---

[116] "HS Student's Social-Media-Fueled Campaign ... - Mashable." 23 Nov.

Robocall, because whatever your opponents throw at you, I categorically believe it cannot be worse than what the Syosset School District did to my family and me. And in our case, truth prevailed over lies. Common sense trumped fear; and good triumphed over evil. **I promise you, that if you stay calm, stay focused, and share the truth, you will be able to handle whatever adversity comes your way as well.**

Election Day

So we've finally made it to the main event, Election Day! **I know in the movies, the presidential candidates are all sitting on the couches, just chilling. But this should not be you!** Local races often come down to just a one vote differential. Don't believe me? Syosset School Board candidate Chris DiFilippo tied candidate Bill Weiner this past May, and won by only one vote after affidavit ballots were counted.[117]

So what do you do? For me, I started my day at the train station, greeting commuters and reminding them to go out and vote if they hadn't already. I then grabbed breakfast, took my cell phone, and sent a text message to every single one of my contacts, asking them to come out and vote. I also sent a Facebook message to every one of my friends who I hadn't already contacted. I can't tell you how many of my friends responded with, "Today's the Election!?" **Every single vote counts. Get your supporters to the polls!** In New York, as

---

2015 <http://mashable.com/2012/05/21/josh-lafazan-social-media/>
[117] "Longwood to have runoff vote while Syosset announces ..." 2015. 26 Nov. 2015 <http://www.newsday.com/long-island/longwood-to-have-runoff-vote-while-syosset-announces-winner-of-3rd-seat-on-school-board-1.10460547>

in most states, there's no *politicking* within 100 feet of the polling place.[118] So what did I do? This May, I had volunteers hold up a huge "Feldman, Lafazan & Hart" banner on the front lawn of the resident across the street from the school (major thank you to the Rametra family). This was further than 100 feet, and every single voter who turned into the school's parking lot to go vote first had to see my campaign banner!

Doug Pascarella, a fellow New Yorker, was keenly aware of the "100 feet" rule. So he got creative as well. Plainedge had just one polling place, so on Election Day, "I pulled my car up...and handed out flyers." Doug jokes that he was, "Actually in school during the vote...I had at least one test that day...I went outside and handed out flyers during my lunch period, and from 2 p.m. until the polls closed I stayed and handed out flyers." Doug is a prime example of giving your campaign everything you have until literally the last possible second.

Like Doug and I, Saira Blair took a similar approach. She recalls how she, "Had a lot of people helping me hold up signs during Primary and Election Days...it was a fun way for them to help out, and I bought them dinner" to say thank you. She continues, "It was a hard day...12 hours in front of a polling place, 84 degrees during the primary, and 40 during the general...neither were particularly enjoyable, but my friends were great." **Your friends will be there for you when you call; don't be afraid to ask for their help.**

[118] "State-laws-polling-place-electioneering-102912." 2013. 26 Nov. 2015 <https://www.supportthevoter.gov/files/2013/12/state-laws-polling-place-electioneering-102912.pdf>

Election Night

It's finally over. You've poured blood, sweat, and tears into your campaign. You turned something that was just a pipe dream into a reality. First and foremost, you should be so proud of yourself. **You've done something that so few people do nationwide— put themselves out there to serve their communities.** Now all you have to do is wait until the results are announced. Something I advise each candidate to do is to write two speeches before the results are announced; one if they win, and one if they lose. In both cases, you're going to want to thank all those who helped you as well as the community for their support. And make sure to thank your family; I can't stress how much a political campaign is a family affair. Remember that nobody likes a sore winner; be gracious in your victory speech, and talk about all the great things you want to do for your community. **But the primary reason I advise you to write two speeches is because often, whether it's in sports or business or politics, people speak and act based off emotions when they lose.** And it's unfortunate that, even though these remarks and actions are not emblematic of the person they are, people often get labeled by this for life. Look no further than the Ohio State football player who gave the middle finger to the fandom of the Big House after being ejected from a game in 2013.[119] I want to stress two important things. **First, if you win, the work has just begun.** You've won your race; now go show the people who put you in office why you deserve to be

---

[119] "Ohio State Michigan Fight 2013 Hall Flips off fans! - YouTube." 2013. 26 Nov. 2015 <https://www.youtube.com/watch?v=db1WWYR2eGU>

there. **Secondly, if you lost, it is the furthest thing from the end of the world.** I can't tell you how many elected officials are currently in office after losing a race. If you don't believe me, I'll name an elected official with pretty high name recognition: The 44th President of the United States, Barack Obama.[120]

---

[120] "In 2000, a Streetwise Veteran Schooled a Bold Young Obama." 2007. 26 Nov. 2015
<http://www.nytimes.com/2007/09/09/us/politics/09obama.html?page wanted=all>

Tips

#1 Deadlines, deadlines, deadlines! Every elected official in this book had to collect signatures on a nominating petition (the amount of signatures required varies by the size of the office you seek), and had to file that petition by a certain date to become a candidate on the ballot. Find out when those deadlines are! Call your district, your town or county, or the board of elections and mark these dates down. Unlike a deadline for a paper which a teacher can move back, these deadlines are non-negotiable. Don't take yourself out of the game for silly negligence.

#2 I found that knocking on doors was a great way to gather signatures. If your election is nonpartisan, you can knock on any home to gather a signature; if your election is partisan, you're going to want to knock on the doors of registered voters in your party. You can receive this information from your country's board of elections.

#3 Internships for high school students are also a great way to get motivated young people involved in your campaigns. High school students are in need of community service and experiences to put on their resumes for college. So rather than working in the district office for a congressman making phone calls or sending letters, you can offer a much more compelling and personal experience. Whereas interns see a congressman maybe once during their entire internship, your interns can work directly with you. Just make sure to let them know you'll write them a letter of recommendation for college—you should always go the extra mile to help those who helped you.

#4 If you're using a regular email service, a trick I was taught is to put your entire list in the "bcc" column, and simply put yourself in the "to" column. Doing this means your recipients don't see the other addresses on your email list, and therefore your opponents can't steal your list and use it for their own campaign.

Chapter Summary

-**You've won your race; now go show the people who put you in office why you deserve to be there.** Secondly, if you lost, it is the furthest thing from the end of the world. I can't tell you how many elected officials are currently in office after losing a race. If you don't believe me, I'll name an elected official with pretty high name recognition: The 44th President of the United States, Barack Obama.[121]

-**When adversity strikes, in that moment, you have to be the calmest, and the most focused.** If we would have panicked, or thrown our hands in the air and given up, I wouldn't be here writing this book right now. But instead, we gathered our composure, took a collective deep breath, and only then, did we take action.

-**Money in an election does not guarantee a winner, and the lack of it doesn't guarantee a loser.** There are things money can buy, and there are things money cannot—truly being a "man of the people" like Marcus Molinaro is, and speaking to residents while knocking on every door three times in your community is something that you just can't buy.

-**Never underestimate the ability of social media.** Through Facebook and Twitter, we were given a platform to share our side of the story. And it quickly spread like wildfire. However, social media can also be a negative. As Chase Harrison says, "Cleanse and lock

---

[121] "In 2000, a Streetwise Veteran Schooled a Bold Young Obama." 2007. 26 Nov. 2015 <http://www.nytimes.com/2007/09/09/us/politics/09obama.html?pagewanted=all>

up all social media accounts. If someone is looking for dirt on you, they will find innocent things and project them as examples of your immaturity."

Impact on Your Life

Author Peter Drucker once said that, "Rank does not confer privilege or give power. It imposes responsibility."[122]

Drucker's words are a code to live by when you take the Oath of Office. Your rank as an elected official does not give you *power;* rather, it gives you *ability.* This isn't *House of Cards,* and you won't become Frank Underwood with his motto that, "The road to power is paved with hypocrisy, and casualties."[123] You have the *ability* to make a difference. You have the *ability* to make your voice heard. And you have the *ability* to make heard the voices of others.

But this attitude that an elected office comes with *power* is exactly the type of insane arrogance that make our current elected officials so unpopular. It's no wonder that, according to *Public Policy Polling*, Congress has a lower approval rating than cockroaches, Genghis Khan, traffic jams, and even Nickelback.[124]

---

[122] "Rank Does Not Confer Privilege or Give Power; It Imposes ..." 2014. 28 Nov. 2015 <http://www.huffingtonpost.com/avril-brikkels/rank-does-not-confer-privilege-or-give-power-it-imposes-responsibility_b_5770826.html>

[123] "Frank Underwood's 15 Best Quotes from House of Cards." 2014. 28 Nov. 2015 <http://parade.com/264672/ashleighschmitz/frank-underwoods-15-best-quotes-from-house-of-cards/>

[124] "Congress somewhere below cockroaches, traffic jams, and ..." 2013. 28 Nov. 2015 2015 <http://www.publicpolicypolling.com/main/2013/01/congress-somewhere-below-cockroaches-traffic-jams-and-nickleback-in-americans-esteem.html>

When you speak, you are no longer speaking as a private citizen; you are speaking as a holder of your elected office. So something I learned when I first took office, and I definitely advise you to do as well, is to use a disclaimer, whether you're giving a speech or writing an opinion piece, stating that you're speaking on behalf of yourself and yourself only. For example, on the school board, only the president can speak on behalf of the board. So through this disclaimer, nobody can ever insinuate that I am speaking on behalf of my colleagues.

Keep in mind that you do not *lose* any privileges after you are elected. Often times I have found that young elected officials will hesitate to say something or do something because of the office they now hold. You maintain every single privilege that you had when you were a private citizen; you simply now, as Drucker infers, have more responsibility with your new rank.

This responsibility will be a major change to your life, especially if you're a teenager like I was—this was a drastic world shift for me. I went from sleeping in on Saturdays and playing video games with friends, to early weekend mornings in Dunkin Donuts pouring through board documents, and meeting my buddies for a late bite at 11:00 p.m. after back-to-back functions.

Being an elected official, you're no longer just accountable to yourself. Since being elected, Mark Kremer shares that, "Well, the responsibility has increased immensely....I measure my responsibility in this office by what I can do for the people." And this responsibility manifests itself in many different ways.

You're responsible to be responsive. Gone are the days of receiving an email on Monday and

saying to yourself, "I'll respond to it after I get done
with my test on Friday." Because the majority of your
job is constituent casework. The Congressional
Research Office defines constituent casework as, "In a
congressional office, the term casework refers to the
response or services that Members of Congress provide
to constituents who request assistance."[125] In short,
your role is to field problems from your constituents
and find them a solution. This requires responsiveness
in a timely manner.

**You're responsible to keep things
confidential.** Now, you may be reading this and
saying "duhh." But board members absolutely have
disclosed confidential matters in the past. And Robert
J. Freeman, Executive Director of the New York State
Committee on Open Government, made very clear in a
memo that, "At this juncture, I note that a ruling by the
Commissioner of Education indicates that members of
a board of education who breach confidentiality of an
executive session may be removed from office."[126] When
you receive information that's confidential, it goes in a
vault, both literally and figuratively. Any confidential
information I hear gets put in my imaginary Fort Knox,
and only gets opened when I step into an executive
session—"Executive sessions are confidential and topics
are only generally noted in open meeting minutes."[127]
And any confidential documents I receive do not get left

---

[125] "Casework in a Congressional Office: Background, Rules ..." 2013. 29
Nov. 2015 <https://www.fas.org/sgp/crs/misc/RL33209.pdf>
[126] "4489 - Welcome to the Committee on Open Government." 2012. 29
Nov. 2015 <http://docs.dos.ny.gov/coog/otext/o4489.htm>
[127] "Executive Session Defined - Davis-Stirling.com." 2014. 29 Nov. 2015
<http://www.davis-
stirling.com/MainIndex/ExecutiveSessionDefined/tabid/1769/Default.as
px>

around the house casually, or thrown into the back of my car, or thrown out in the garbage when I'm done reading them; they go into a folder in my briefcase, and get shredded when I want to dispose of them.

You're responsible to behave a certain way. You are now a role model in your community, and not just for the youth; you should strive to be an example of the way everyone should live: with honesty, integrity, and dignity. The first time I really felt this responsibility happened when I was with a group of my Syosset High School classmates at the On Parade Diner in Woodbury during my first month on the board. The election was just a few weeks prior, and as I entered the diner I was recognized and greeted by about a dozen people as I made my way to my table. As the group I was with sat down to order, I felt three of the kids were acting quite inappropriately. They were, unaware to my knowledge before I arrived, under the influence of alcohol, and were using loud and profane language that was making a scene. It was a Saturday night, which meant the diner was quite crowded, and I made the decision to leave. I didn't want to be, as unfortunately is the case often, guilty by association. Here it was, just a month prior, and I would have looked at these drunk idiots and laughed, not considering that my sitting at their table associated them with me. But you now have a responsibility to be a role model, and since the image I want to portray to the public is one of consideration and maturity, my responsibility trumps hanging out with certain friends in certain settings.

Lastly, and arguably most importantly, you're responsible to actually do something. You are not elected to collect a paycheck, show up at fairs and functions, and smile for the cameras; you are there to fight for those issues on your platform, and to deliver reforms for your constituents. In fact, this was the first

area of disagreement I had when I first took office back
in 2012 with some of my friends who either held elected
office, or worked in government. Essentially the whole
world told me that I should just sit quietly and listen
during my first year on the board—that I should just
learn my first year, and then I'd be ready to act my
second year. Clearly I didn't listen, as my actions at my
second ever public monthly board meeting defending
my right to speak led *Newsday* to print the headline
<u>Syosset School Board President Threatens to Quit</u>.[128] I
felt that, after having been just elected with a clear and
loud mandate from the people, I had a responsibility to
do something. I had a responsibility to deliver change.
And if I couldn't achieve success with these reforms,
then at the very least I had a responsibility to *fight*. **As I
said before, I'm a fighter; I'm hyper-passionate,
and don't know any other way to operate.**

I want to make a promise to you, so listen
closely—you *can* do this. You're just as capable as any
adult to serve your community. And if at any time you
doubt whether you can handle the job, heed Mark
Kremer's advice: **"Put me in over my head, and
watch me swim to the top."**

But in my opinion, the biggest impact on your
life will be the sacrifices you make, both as a candidate
and an elected official.

Chris Scales says that **"Being a public figure
makes me very cautious of every move that I
make and say. I was well aware of all of this
before I submitted my petition."** Seldom has
somebody articulated quite the way I feel before I heard
this from Chris.

---

[128] "Syosset School Board president threatens to quit | Newsday." 2012.
28 Nov. 2015 <http://www.newsday.com/long-island/nassau/syosset-
school-board-president-threatens-to-quit-1.3887381>

I'm often asked why I don't drink. Sure, now that I'm of age, I'll have the occasional strawberry daiquiri when I find myself on a beach somewhere. But 360 days out of the year, I don't drink. And it's not because I take a medicine that gets upset by alcohol, or because it's against my religion; it's a conscious life choice I make. The reason? In the 21st century, the age where everybody has a smart phone and is constantly recording each other, saying one wrong thing is the difference between a bright political future and resignation–the difference between getting to continue to wake up each morning and have the best job in the world, and having it all taken away from me. So I choose to always be cognizant of what I say, where I am, and the company I keep. I opt to always maintain full control over my body, mind and actions. And I do this by always being sober, and not under the influence of alcohol.

This all sounds pretty reasonable, right? Except for the fact that I get constantly ridiculed by *everybody*. Whenever I choose not to drink, it's always a consistent barrage of comments and judgments hurled my way. Remember when I spoke earlier about doing things *differently,* and how it freaks people out? This is exhibit A.

I highlight this for two reasons. First, that "stomach of steel" we developed? It's not just for the campaign–it should be used in your everyday life, whenever you want to do something differently, or take a different path. Secondly, I am the exception, not the rule. This is simply the way I choose to live my life–in fact, the vast majority of elected officials don't abstain from alcohol. I highlight this as an example of a life choice I make, and to remind you that you should take a little from everybody in this book to create your own style. There is no blueprint for what sacrifices you have to make. Rather, it's something you have to decide on your own. **However it's those individuals who are prepared to make these sacrifices that are the ones who excel in office.** Look no further than Congressman Paul Ryan, who even as Speaker of the House, continues to sleep on a cot in his congressional office so that he may work longer hours.[129]

For Jon Fiore, life as an elected official has affected him on campus. He shares that, "The biggest impact that this has had on me is undoubtedly in my college experience. **Fully understanding that I am now a public figure, I often have to choose to decline to attend certain social events that I know are likely to lead to trouble or unethical behaviors.** I constantly find myself on my best behavior because I know how much I have to lose."

This is an incredibly mature outlook, and I have full appreciation for what Jon is talking about as it applies to my life as well.

I'll never forget meeting Saira Blair in Austin Texas this year, and discussing the sacrifices accompanying our jobs. I was joking that I had the world's worst high school spring break. Almost all of my friends either went to a resort in the Bahamas, or they were players on the lacrosse team and went to Disney World for a tournament. I spent the entire week of my high school spring break knocking on doors and collecting signatures, and I still commiserate with Greg Morley and Justin Cristando to this day how we spent every single night at Hurricane Grill in Syosset because we had nothing better to do. I couldn't believe that Saira actually one-upped me. Saira, who campaigned

[129] "Even as House Speaker, Paul Ryan Sleeps in His Office ..." 27 Nov. 2015 <http://www.nytimes.com/2015/11/11/us/politics/speaker-paul-ryan-sleeps-in-office.html>

during her senior year in high school as well, says she, **"Had to miss both my proms in order to participate in youth in government."** She continues saying that she, "Had to give up time spent at movies, writing hand written letters to send to potential voters."

For me, my sacrifices started with my college decision. While all my friends were applying to out-of-state four-year schools, I chose to stay home and attend Nassau Community College on Long Island. I did this because I knew the fight against the superintendent, as well as the entrenched incumbents, would be incredibly difficult, and by being home I would be able to best effect the changes I wished to make. Flash forward two years later, after the retirement of our superintendent, there came another sacrifice. I gained admission into Cornell University, a 253-mile trip from my house in Woodbury. **So I sacrifice my weekends at college, spending the week in my dorm room, and commuting back home to Syosset about 3 weekends a month to attend the monthly board meetings, community events, and to meet with concerned residents.** Jake Asman and Dan Budick have even dubbed me "Cornell's first commuter student from Long Island." But I drive those long nights on Route 17, missing out on campus life, because my first and most important priority is, and will continue to be, my constituents. In fact, during my re-election campaign, I drove home from Cornell every weekend from February through May. True story–the guy manning the drive-thru window at Taco Bell off Exit 101 told me I was single handedly stimulating their local economy.

But the sacrifices I make extend far outside my college campus. It affects the company I keep. It affects the places I choose to go. It affects the life I live.

Because I believe that our elected officials should behave like they are worthy of serving in public office. And if I believe elected officials should lead by example, then I better be setting a good example myself.

Often times when things get difficult, and I feel those around me just don't understand what I'm going through, I turn to those in this book. I have found that most people just won't have appreciation for the sacrifices you make, to no fault of their own. Which is why those interviewed in this book have become some of my closest friends; when you experience something yourself, you're more sensitive to it. In this vein, once again please do NOT be afraid to reach out to the elected officials in this book. We all went through what you will go through. We all live our lives in a similar fashion. **And we always choose to *collaborate* rather than *compete*.** When one of us gets elected, it's a boost to the entire Millennial generation; it's one more of our voices that gets to be heard in the halls of government. I joke that similar to the movie *Wanted,* where there was a fraternity of trained assassins, young elected officials are like a fraternity as well. But like in the movie *Wanted,* we take care of our own.

Being an elected official will have a profound impact on your life. You are no longer just a private citizen; you are now a public servant. And those who can't discern, or don't appreciate the vast dichotomy between the two are those who don't last in this business.

Mark Kremer sums this transition up best, saying, "I don't belong to just myself anymore." But Mark continues, "I like that. Myself along with my time are devoted to the people I represent." This is the crux of the job—devoting yourself, your time, and your resources to those around you. If you can do this, you're going to be great.

So is all of this worth it? Is the added responsibility worth it? Are the sacrifices worth it? Are the changes to your life worth it? Saira Blair emphatically says, "Definitely!" Many others agree.

My answer in short is this—being an elected official has been the greatest privilege of my short life, and I'm thankful each and every day for all of the added responsibility, all of the sacrifices, and all of the changes to my life. Because all of this had led me to the life I lead today—one where I get to wake up each morning and make an impact in my community. **Muhammad Ali once said that, "Service to others is the rent you pay for your room here on earth."[130] Having gotten a taste of public service, I guess I'll be a renter forever.**

---

[130] "Service to others is the rent you pay for your room here on ..." 2003. 29 Nov. 2015 <http://www.brainyquote.com/quotes/quotes/m/muhammadal136676.html>

<u>Tips</u>

#1 When you speak, you are no longer speaking as a private citizen; you are speaking as a holder of your elected office. So something I learned when I first took office, and I definitely advise you to do as well, is to use a disclaimer, whether you're giving a speech or writing an opinion piece, stating that you're speaking on behalf of yourself and yourself only. For example, on the school board, only the president can speak on behalf of the board. So through this disclaimer, nobody can ever insinuate that I am speaking on behalf of my colleagues.

#2 Do NOT be afraid to reach out to the elected officials in this book. We all went through what you will go through. We all live our lives in a similar fashion. And we always choose to *collaborate* rather than *compete*. When one of us gets elected, it's a boost to the entire Millennial generation; it's one more of our voices that gets to be heard in the halls of government. I joke that similar to the movie *Wanted*, where there was a fraternity of trained assassins, young elected officials are like a fraternity as well. But like in the movie *Wanted*, we take care of our own.

#3 Before you take the Oath of Office, be prepared to make sacrifices in your life for your new position as an elected official. Because it's those individuals who are prepared to make these sacrifices that are the ones who excel in office. Look no further than Congressman Paul Ryan, who even as Speaker of the House, continues to sleep on a cot in his congressional office so that he may work longer hours.

#4 If you are a student in high school, think about how serving in your position will impact your college decision. I knew that, with Dr. Hankin as Syosset's Superintendent, in order to best serve my constituents I had to stay home, and therefore only applied to Nassau Community College.

Chapter Summary

-So is all of this worth it? Is the added responsibility worth it? Are the sacrifices worth it? Are the changes to your life worth it? Saira Blair emphatically says, "Definitely!" Many others agree. My answer in short is this—being an elected official has been the greatest privilege of my short life, and I'm thankful each and every day for all of the added responsibility, all of the sacrifices, and all of the changes to my life. Because all of this had led me to the life I lead today—one where I get to wake up each morning and make an impact in my community. Muhammad Ali once said that, "Service to others is the rent you pay for your room here on earth." Having gotten a taste of public service, I guess I'll be a renter forever.

-Your rank as an elected official does not give you *power*; rather, it gives you *ability*. You have the *ability* to make a difference. You have the *ability* to make your voice heard. And you have the *ability* to make heard the voices of others. But this attitude that an elected office comes with *power* is exactly the type of insane arrogance that make our current elected officials so unpopular. It's no wonder that, according to *Public Policy Polling*, Congress has a lower approval rating than cockroaches, Genghis Khan, traffic jams, and even Nickelback.

-I want to make a promise to you, so listen closely—you *can* do this. You're just as capable as any adult to serve your community. And if at any time you doubt whether you can handle the job, heed Mark Kremer's advice: "Put me in over my head, and watch me swim to the top."

Lessons Learned

Between the elected officials in this book, you have at your disposal over a century of experience serving in public elected office. The questions asked to those interviewed for this book varied, but I always ended the interview with one final question—what advice do you have for young people looking to get involved in politics? I think there's no better way to end the book then to share the answers I received.

Saira Blair

Saira Blair leads by example when she advises young people looking to get involved in politics to, "Start at the local level." She says that, **"Most people, when they think politics, think national…you have so much going on around you in your hometown and home state…this is what will affect you the most."** She stresses the importance of thinking local, continuing that you should, "Really try to stay away from watching the news as much as possible…you get caught up in it, and it's more important to stay as informed as possible on what's happening close to home." Lastly, she feels it's important to, "Find a mentor that ran for office, and learn as much as possible…I have a few role models who I really look up to, and without them I would be lost… at any age, it's great to have people to talk to, and to give you advice on anything."

Ian Calderon

Ian Calderon had a lot of doubters in his ear when he ran, and that's why he says, "First, don't listen to anyone who tells you that you can't do it...People told me I couldn't do it because I was young." But his biggest piece of advice revolves around owning your youth. He shares, **"My biggest piece of advice for young people is that you're young. If you truly feel you can have an impact in office, you need to do it. If you win, look at what you get to be a part of. And if you lose, what are you really losing? You have the ability to shoot for the stars because you're young...if running for office is your dream, now is your time."** Ian definitely had major FOMO (for our older readers, FOMO is an acronym for fear of missing out), and shares that he, "Never wanted to be a person where I looked back and said 'what if' I ran," and that this feeling, "Happens during the campaign when you want to quit...Even in losing you still win, the people you've met, the skills you've learned, the things you've accomplished." And, "If you win–GREAT, you get to make a difference." Lastly, he says emphatically that, "We need the next generation that will be responsible for our seniors to get involved...if we want the world to be a certain way, we need to decide it...we need to be the ones to make those choices."

Justin Chenette

When he ran, Justin Chenette had a great mentor in now–State Senator Linda Valentino, so it's no surprise that he advises you to, **"Find one person that you can really trust, will be there for support, and has years of experience."** Justin is a rare breed, as he's truly "color-blind" when it comes to the political parties of others. He says to, "Focus on non-partisan activities within your campaign structure...You don't have a lot of time to talk to people when door knocking, so community service-like projects within your campaign brings people to your campaign, and the level of awareness transcends beyond the Republican or Democratic label." He says you should, "Purposely try to go above and beyond...people always saw me in the community, and instead of just attending, I would be volunteering...Involvement counters all negativity about young people being lazy, and frames your personal brand." Like Saira, he feels it's important to, "Reach out to people in office, figure out what being in office means, and understand what you actually want to accomplish. Your answer should never be because you want to run and it looks fun." Lastly, he shares that, "If at any point your campaign is more about you than helping people, it's not a good idea."

Daniel Croson

Many people will tell you to wait until you're older to run for office. Not Daniel Croson. **When asked what his advice was to young people looking to get involved in politics, he said frankly, "Do it now." He believes there are, "A million reasons to wait until you're older...our generation is underrepresented" right now.** Candidates often feel they can't run because they're not a "Bush" or a "Clinton" in their local community. Daniel disagrees with this thinking, and strongly asserts that, "Nobody has a right to a position." He shares that, "My candidacy inspired other people...just the fact that I would knock on people's doors and ask them for their vote, people much older would commend me for running for office." He feels that elected office, "Provides a vehicle where people can channel their desire for change...if you see somebody involved, it inspires you to get more involved."

Tom DiNapoli

If anybody had a tough road to elected office, it was Tom DiNapoli; he was trying to do something that literally no one had done before. So I take Tom at his word when he shares, "I don't think they should be intimidated. Access [to office] is easier than people realize." He feels that, "Starting at the local level, such as running for your local school board of education, a village trustee seat, the library board, is a great way to start." And Tom says that elected office is not your only option for an introduction to politics. He notes the Big Apple as an example, saying that, "New York City has community boards you can get appointed to...if it's not elected than an advisory board is a way for people to start to get to know you, and for you to get familiar with issues." He also points out that these, "Positions tend to be non-partisan," which is a great way for you to make friends on both sides of the aisle. Like Daniel Croson, Das Williams, and so many others in this book, Tom advises you to, "Help other candidates get involved." Lastly, Tom mentions a very important piece of advice— you can only be a representative for the area in which you reside. In this regard, Tom says to, **"Decide where you see your community...will you live where you grow up, or live somewhere else when you're done with your schooling...decide where you're going to reside," before you seek elected office.**

Anthony Fasano

Anthony Fasano was quite similar to Ian Calderon, during his race, in that he had a myriad of doubters who thought he didn't stand a chance. In this realm, Anthony says, **"Don't be intimidated by people who say you can't do it...the law says in essence that if you want to get involved, if you're a citizen, and over 18, you can do it."** He recalls how, "When word started spreading that I would run, people reached out and said don't do this...just live your life like a normal college student, small town politics is hard...I didn't believe in that. If I listened to those people, I wouldn't be where I am today, and our district wouldn't be where it is today." Anthony was a football player, so he knows that nobody just hands you anything; you have to go out and earn playing time, you have to fight through blocks to make the tackle, and so on and so forth. Thus Anthony concludes by saying, "Your strongest advocate should be yourself."

Jon Fiore

Ronald Reagan said to, "Trust, but verify." Jon Fiore shares this same type of vigilance, sharing that, **"My first two words of advice would be to 'be careful.' Politics is indeed a dangerous game and you can make enemies just as quickly as you can make new friends."** Jon notes that as an elected official, you are no longer just acting on behalf of yourself. He feels that, "It is necessary to realize that your actions will also have an impact on other people, sometimes more so than you realize; what seems insignificant to you may mean the world to someone else. Also, one must realize that once the decision is made to enter the political arena, from that point on, you are in the public eye and people expect you to behave in a certain manner." Jon warns young candidates that they should not run unless they are sure that they are *ready* for the commitment of holding that office. He says, "In my opinion, I think the most important thing young people need to be careful of is getting involved too early. Although a person may feel that they are mature and capable enough to get involved at such a young age, the fact of the matter is that in most cases, they truly are not. I do not believe that I can stress this point enough. When young people erroneously decide to run for office without fully understanding the implications of their actions, it leads to the public forming a poor opinion of other young adults that wish to be a part of the world of public service."

Cyrus Habib

Cyrus Habib is adamant that Millennials everywhere need to join community organizations, and that it is these organizations that are a precursor to building your "civic resume." He says community organizations are, "Dying to have young people involved...get on the board of any non-profit that matches your values: parks' board, planning commission...build that civic resume." This concept of a "civic resume" is vital to establishing your credibility as a young person seeking elected office. Cyrus feels that, "Voters want to see it [civic resume], you'll learn more, and you'll develop your list of community endorsers that are especially important when you're young." He uses the example of a school superintendent as a possible community endorser. Cyrus explains that, "To have the superintendent of schools to support you as an early candidate for the board of education is a really great endorsement...you get that endorsement because you volunteered on a committee, etc...., putting yourself in a great spot." **Lastly, Cyrus advises young candidates to plan their forays into political life far in advance. Cyrus says that, "I think that people view running for office as the first step...it's really the third step...be strategic, and spend a couple of years positioning yourself." He continues, "Don't run this year, run in two years, and spend these two years getting yourself out there...don't run now, set the stage."**

Chase Harrison

Chase Harrison says that if you should be prepared for one thing during your time in office, "Be prepared for frustration. If you are young and trying to get involved, you have to be better than others in the field to compensate for your age." But Chase, like Ian, advises you NOT to run away from your youth. He says, **"Don't disown your age. Don't try to act like an adult and don't take yourself too seriously. When I see teenagers acting like professional politicians, I find it uncomfortable. No one expects you to act like a 40 year old. Understand that young politicians are more innocent, can be less serious, and can provide key insight that adults cannot. Play up your age as an advantage and not as a liability."** Lastly, like any new relationship, there inevitably will be friction and discomfort with the people you will begin working with. Chase recalls that, "As my term went on and I proved I wasn't just a rabble-rouser, I began to gain the trust of the superintendent and several board members. This certainly made being on the board a more enjoyable experience." This story goes to show that if you work hard, and if people can see that you're undoubtedly serving for the right reasons, people may not come to like you, but they will come to *respect* you.

Mark Kremer

Mark Kremer has a pretty profound expression that he uses in his own life, and it's something I've since adopted in mine as well. **Whenever people doubt Mark's ability to live up to a challenge, he counters, "Put me in over my head, and watch me swim to the top."** When it comes to running for office, Mark backs any candidate who has the courage to chase his/her dreams with the ferocity that it demands. Mark shares that, "If you are really serious about it then go for it. Never be afraid to chase what you are passionate about, whether it is politics or anything else. Live your dreams."

Connor Kurtz

There's a common expression that, "Just showing up is half the battle." When I asked Connor Kurtz this question, he fired back with two words— "Show up!" Connor stresses the importance of the voice of youth in politics, saying, **"Do your homework, and never be afraid to contribute to the political process...there are so many opportunities for civic involvement. Just being there and adding your voice to the conversation means so much."** Also, like Tom DiNapoli, he notes that elected office is not the only way to make a difference. He says you, "Don't always need to jump in and run for something...try to influence a discussion, try to guide your community in a positive direction and never sell out your principles." Connor, like myself, shares a distaste for many of the current representatives serving in our government, and thus advises you to, "Stay true to what you are and what you believe. Don't lie, don't cheat, don't steal!" Connor is also a believer that politics is not a lifetime profession, but rather a finite endeavor. He shares that, "This isn't supposed to be something you're entrenched in...If you've accomplished your goals, it's time to let someone else give it a shot...if you're able to implement positive changes, those changes will stay after you're gone."

Nicole Malliotakis

Nicole Malliotakis calls being an elected official, "One of most challenging jobs you can have." Moreover, she warns young candidates that, "you really have to want to do this. You have to have a passion or you won't do a good job." Nicole, an avid *House of Cards* fan, is a pragmatist like Frank Underwood (just not a *ruthless* pragmatist). Therefore she shares that you're, **"Not going to make everybody happy. You have to do what you feel is right all of the time, what's best for people you represent...everyone won't agree with you all the time." She references the late New York City Mayor Ed Koch when he said, "If you agree with me on 9 out of 12 issues, vote for me. If you agree with me on 12 out of 12 issues, see a psychiatrist."** Nicole says you have to have a couple of key characteristics to truly do a good job; you, "Have to be principled, dedicated, and passionate, and put in the effort that it takes...If you really don't want this job you will be terrible at it...you'll be run out of office."

Marcus Molinaro

Marcus Molinaro ran an entire town at the age of 19, and therefore knows better than anyone the importance of preparation in order to best get the job done. He shares that you, **"Have to be that much more prepared than anyone else...I read every page of the Tivoli minutes book from 1872-1995...this took me the entire year I served on the village board."** Mark Twain famously said that, "History doesn't repeat itself, but it does rhyme." Marcus, like Twain, does not take for granted the importance of understanding history, saying that he, "Had to understand how we got to where we were...when someone said 'in 1967 we did this,' I could respond knowledgeably." Marcus advises young politicos to handle adversity with calmness. He says, "Be willing and able to accept criticism without overreacting...be calm, and be empathetic...this minimizes adversity." Lastly, Marcus left me with a great motto for knocking on doors that I used during my campaign; "One door, one hand, one face at a time explaining who I was and why I was prepared to represent them."

Ellen Nesbitt

The doubt surrounding Ellen Nesbitt's candidacy was everywhere, including inside her own house. So Ellen speaks from a position of experience and strength when she says, **"If you feel like it's something you want to do, just go out and do it...If I had really thought about how unrealistic the numbers in my district were, I wouldn't have run."** She continues, "People saw I was passionate when I spoke to them, and responded really well to that." With a 3:1

enrollment disadvantage, many can legitimately say that it was not realistic for Ellen to win on Election Day. But she did. And then she did it again in November of 2015. Therefore she says that, "If there's something, not even just in politics, that you want to do and it doesn't seem realistic, just do it...realistic ideas don't always win."

Doug Pascarella

Doug Pascarella was the president of his class, and therefore was a veteran, rather than a neophyte, in mobilizing the support of his classmates. During his election, he thought to himself, "If I can get all of my classmates registered, there's about 100 votes right there." Doug's strategy is a no-brainer for all young candidates to adopt. Doug advises young people interested in politics to, **"Learn the landscape and then get into it...you have to have a knowledge of how things work before you jump right in, otherwise you'll look like a fool."** In this regard, Doug speaks from personal experience; "When I ran, I went to board of education meetings, knew the key players, and knew who was running." Like Connor referenced, Doug says he, "Did his homework." In short, Doug says that in order to do this, you, "Have to be nerdy."

Brandon Pugh

Brandon Pugh is keenly aware that politics is local, and that your reputation sticks with you. In this regard, he shares that you should, **"Start now regardless of what political or non-partisan office you seek...it doesn't matter if you're 13 or 22, your reputation is key...if they see you're**

active in your community, no matter what your age is it gets your name out and people remember." He contrasts this with the alternative of not getting involved until you begin your campaign. He says, "If you sit home all day and are not active in your community, you're going to have a much tougher time when you run." Brandon speaks from personal experience when he advises young people to, "Get involved immediately if you decide to run and get elected." In addition to his election to his school board, at 21, Brandon was elected as president of the Burlington County School Boards' Association in New Jersey. He implores you to, "Seek opportunities to get involved locally...in the county and state association...seek a committee chairmanship...leverage your youth!"

Chris Scales

From speaking with Chris Scales, I can easily discern his passion for his position on the Hamilton Township Board of Education. Chris shares that, "From just serving in public life for the past six months, I can truly say that it has been one of the most rewarding experiences of my life." He notes that often times young elected officials will take positions that are unpopular, or won't have widespread support, saying that, "I tell others who are considering this path to always remain true to themselves and never stop fighting for what is right, even if it means standing alone." Lastly, Chris advises all young people interested in politics to figure out what they're passionate about, and then to fight to make those things become a reality. **He tells me, "As the late-Senator Paul Wellstone has said, 'If we don't fight hard enough for the things we stand**

for, at some point we have to recognize that we don't really stand for them.'"

Michaelle Solages

Michaelle Solages wants young people in politics to be prepared to both achieve success, and to handle adversity; to weather the ups and the downs of the job. She reflects on her own experience serving in the New York State Assembly, sharing that, "Government, especially in Albany, is fast paced. Every day I learn something new when I'm up there, it's a roller coaster...one day you're on top of the world, and the next day down in the dumps struggling to get everything done." She continues, saying that, "At one point you're able to pass legislation in your House, and the next day you're begging a state senator to use as much passion as I have to pass the bill...then you have to work with the governor." Michaelle believes that slow and steady wins the race, telling me that, "You have to take it a day at a time, plan in advance...you have to have a strategy in your mind, it's all about plan, plan, plan." Lastly, often politics is personal, and this is something Michaelle warns *against*. She advises you to, **"Never take anything personal...at the end of the day you're doing what's right for yourself, and your community, and that's really all that matters."**

Das Williams

Das Williams, like Nicole Malliotakis, stresses the importance of only running for office if you're able to give it nothing short of your all. He says that, "If you're going to run for office, you have to really commit to doing the work. That means making the phone calls

for money and knocking on doors to talk to voters."
Das, having worked on campaigns since he was a
teenager, knows them inside and backwards.
Something he tells me is that there isn't an easy
approach, or a cheat code to use. He shares that,
**"There aren't any shortcuts. It's a lot of work.
But if you're committed to the community you
represent, and making a difference, it's all
worth it.**

Daniel Zolnikov

When Daniel Zolnikov first ran in 2012, little did
he think he would later become a *Forbes 30 Under 30*
honoree, let alone actually *win* his race. In this regard,
he tells me that, "A lot of people don't think they could
ever do it, because they never try." **When Daniel first
explored running, he was talking to some of the
local politicos who summarily told him, "You
have to be really smart to do it." His response?
"No, I'm as normal a person as you, I just
wanted this and I did it."** Daniel emphatically
stresses the importance of accountability, noting there
were, "No excuses," when he ran; "I didn't make up
excuses why I couldn't do it, I just did it" He advises
young people interested in politics to, "Jump on board
of a campaign, get involved, find your way in, figure it
out, and just do it."

So earlier in the book, I told the story of
originally breaking the news to my mom that I wanted
to run for office as a trustee on the Syosset School
Board. Though there was definite hesitation, she told

me, as she always does, "If you're all-in, then we're all-in."

I've worked on this book for about a year now, and have spent many a late night conducting interviews, researching information, and gathering facts to give you what I didn't have when I ran; a comprehensive, 360-degree guide on how to run an impactful campaign and win as a young candidate. The fact that you've made it to the end of my book means the world to me. **In fact it means so much, that I say this to you with all of my heart—if you're all-in, then I'm all-in.** Email me, Facebook me, get in touch with me if you have any questions, need any help, or just want to chat. If you're serious about your race, and truly are running for the *right* reasons, I will have your back 100% and do whatever I can to help you realize your dream.

I'll leave you with this final thought, and a quote that hangs on a poster on the wall of my room at Cornell and that I look at every night before I go to sleep. Too often young candidates are met with the response "that's impossible" when they tell their friends, family, and neighbors about their desire to run for office. I have this to say you—they're wrong. You—without a doubt—*can* do this. **Have the courage of your convictions to move forward with your ideas *regardless* of what your detractors say. Your youth IS your advantage to achieve the impossible. Because as Nelson Mandela says, "It always seems impossible until it's done.**

Quick Links

Lawn Signs- www.ImageGraphic.com

Business Cards- www.VistaPrint.com

Design- www./tinyurl.com/j5vy7dp

Robocalls- www.Robodial.org

Direct Mail- www.USPS.com

Virtual Town Halls- www.Spreecast.com

Website Builder- www.Squarespace.com

Email-www.MailChimp.com

MEET AMERICA'S YOUNG ELECTED OFFICIALS

SAIRA BLAIR
Elected at 18 in 2014 to the West Virginia House of
Delegates
@ElectSairaBlair
(304)-268-2692
SairaBlair@Yahoo.com

IAN CALDERON
Elected at 27 in 2012 to the California State Assembly
@IanCalderon
(916)-319-2057
Assemblymember.Calderon@Assembly.CA.Gov

JUSTIN CHENTTE
Elected at 21 in 2012 to the Maine House of
Representatives
@justinchenette
(207)-590-3266
justinchenette@gmail.com

DANIEL CROSON
Elected at 22 in 2013 to the Carteret School Board of
Education
@danielcroson (Instagram)
(732)-261-8684
danielcroson@gmail.com

THOMAS DiNAPOLI
Elected at 18 in 1972 to the Mineola School Board of
Education
@NYSComptroller
(518)-474-3506
www.osc.state.ny.us

ANTHONY FASANO
Elected at 19 in 2013 to the Hopatcong Board of
Education
@AJFasano
(973)-525-0632
Anthony.Joseph.Fasano@gmail.com

JON FIORE
Elected at 18 in 2014 to the New York Mills Union Free
School District
@jonnyyfi
(315)-534-9186
Jon.m.fiore@gmail.com

CYRUS HABIB
Elected at 31 in 2012 to the Washington House of
Representatives
@CyrusHabib
(360)-786-7694
cyrus.habib@leg.wa.gov

CHASE HARRISON
Elected at 18 in 2013 to the Millburn Board of
Education
@BuenasNochase
(973)-747-6802
ChaseRHarrison@gmail.com

MARK KREMER
Elected at 18 in 2014 to the Southgate Community
Schools Board of Education
@MarkJKremer
(734)-363-0550
markjosephkremer@gmail.com

CONNOR KURTZ
Elected at 18 in 2011 to the Daniel Boone Area Board of
School Directors
@ConnorKurtz
connor@connorkurtz.com

NICOLE MALLIOTAKIS
Elected at 29 in 2010 to the New York State Assembly
@nmalliotakis
(718)-987-0197
malliotakisn@assembly.state.ny.us

MARCUS MOLINARO
Elected at 18 in 1994 to the Village of Tivoli Board of Trustees
@marcmolinaro
(845)-486-2000
marcusmolinaro@gmail.com

ELLEN NESBITT
Elected at 19 in 2013 to the Dutchess County Legislator
@ell3nnicole
(845)-416 8415
ellennesbitt94@gmail.com

DOUG PASCARELLA
Elected at 18 in 2004 to the Plainedge School Board of
Education
@dougpascarella
(516)-581-3039
douglas.j.pascarella@gmail.com

BRANDON PUGH
Elected at 19 in 2012 to the Moorestown Board of
Education
@Brandon_J_Pugh
(856)-214-2929
bpugh@brandonjpugh.com

CHRIS SCALES
Elected at 18 in 2014 to the Hamilton Township District Board of Education
@Chris_scales1
(609)-213-5103
Christopher.scales1@gmail.com

MICHAELLE SOLAGES
Elected at 27 in 2012 to the New York State
Assembly
@MichaelleSolage
(516)-366-0522
ms@MichaelleSolages.com

DAS WILLIAMS
Elected at 29 in 2003 to the Santa Barbara City Council
@DasWilliams
(916) 319-2037
http://asmdc.org/members/a37/

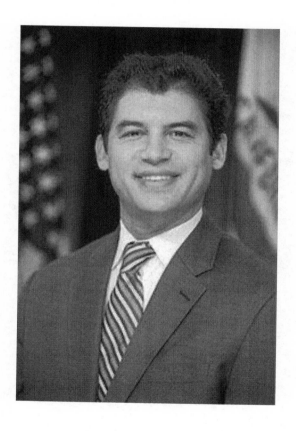

DANIEL ZOLNIKOV
Elected at 25 in 2012 to the Montana House of
Representatives
@DanielZolnikov
(406)-861-5210
Daniel.Zolnikov@gmail.com

About the Author

In May of 2012, at 18 years old, Joshua A.
Lafazan became one of the youngest elected officials in
the history of New York State when he received 82% of
the vote to earn a seat on the Syosset School Board of
Education. At the time of the election, Joshua was
senior class president scheduled to graduate a month
later from Syosset High School, a North Shore Long
Island, New York hamlet with 6,600 students. In
December of 2013, Joshua earned an Associate Degree
in Arts from the Honors' Program at Nassau
Community College on Long Island. Joshua continued
his education at the Cornell University ILR School,
pursuing a Bachelor of Science in Industrial and Labor
Relations with a May 2016 graduation date. Joshua has
received various awards for his work both on the
Syosset School Board and in the Syosset community.
The *Syosset Patch*, a hyper-local news organization
from AOL, selected Joshua as "The Person Who
Mattered Most in 2011." In 2012, Joshua was named to
the *Long Island Press's* Power List of "The 50 Most
Influential People on Long Island," and was named by
Red Alert Politics as one of their "30 Under 30" on their

national list. In 2014, Joshua received the Academy of Education Arts and Sciences Educators' Voice Award for "School Board Member of the Year," and most recently, Joshua received the New York State School Board's Association "Board Mastery Award" in 2015.

Website- www.JoshLafazan.com

Twitter- @JoshuaLafazan

Email- JoshLafazan@gmail.com

Made in the USA
Charleston, SC
10 December 2015